Anger Management for Parents

3 BOOKS IN 1

How to Manage Your Emotions & Raise a Happy and Confident Child.

Includes Emotional Intelligence for Women & Men + Critical Thinking for kids and teens.

COURTNEY MIRIAM GARCIA

Description 7

Introduction 9

Chapter 1. Identifying Triggers 11

Chapter 2. Signs and symptoms of anger and the chronic anger .. 17

Chapter 3. How Anger Can Damage People Around You 21

Chapter 4. Why is Being Angry Very Unhealthy? 27

Chapter 5. Positive Ways to Express Anger 34

Chapter 6. How to Control Your Anger without Drugs 41

Chapter 7. Communication and Anger Management 44

Chapter 8. How to Deal with Stress to Get Rid of Anger 48

Chapter 9. Using Anger for Good 61

Chapter 10. How to Shift Your Perceptions to Lower Your Anger 70

Chapter 11. Anger Counselling 72

Chapter 12. The Humble Approach 80

Chapter 13. Simple Anger Management Techniques 83

Chapter 14. Anger and lifestyle 87

Chapter 15. Taming Toddler Tantrums - Ideas That Work 92

Chapter 16. Anger Management Test 94

BOOK 1

Introduction 215

Chapter 1. What is the Concept of Anger Management? 222

Chapter 2. Who is Dad in the Family? 228

Chapter 3. Raising a Lively Child or Children 235

Chapter 4. Reason Why Dads Get Angry with Their Children 242

Chapter 5. Dad's Anger Issues Vs. Mom's Anger Issues 248

Chapter 6. The Ramifications of Dad's Anger 255

Chapter 7. How Dads Cope Up With Anger Towards their Children 262

Chapter 8. Controlling Dad's Angry Outbursts 269

Chapter 9. Guide to Anger Management Regimen 276

Conclusion 282

Description 105

Introduction 107

Chapter 1. Types of Anger 111

Chapter 2. Signs You Are Struggling with Anger 117

Chapter 3. Checklist For Anger Detection 121

Chapter 4. Reasons for Anger Management 130

Chapter 5. Using Psychology to Treat Anger 138

Chapter 6. Mental Health and Anger 141

Chapter 7. Anger Counseling 146

Chapter 8. How To Get To The Root Of Your Anger 155

Chapter 9. Positive Self-Talk 161

Chapter 10. Techniques To Calm You Down When You're Angry
.... 168

Chapter 11. The Biggest Mistakes Of Anger Management 182

Chapter 12. Solid Tips For Boosting Emotional Self-Awareness . 188

Chapter 13. Tips For Anger Management 197

Conclusion 212

Chapter 17. Outcomes 99

Chapter 18. Connect your emotions with values 101

Conclusion 103

you can get rid of these complex problems is through proper anger management programs and initiatives.

This is how you will learn to control your anger when faced with an unwanted situation. In this book, we have highlighted the various ways in which you can detect that you have anger issues. We have also highlighted how you can deal with that anger to keep at bay. Therefore, it is up to you to take the necessary actions so that you can deal with anger issues and enjoy a happy and healthy life. Good luck!

Description

Indeed, anger is something that is very serious and can affect the people around us and us. What you have to notice here is the fact that the initial adverse effect of skipping anger management is that you will soon forget self-control. The feelings of anger may start to make you feel as though you are falling off the edge. Then you start feeling that small things aggravate and distress you. Things that would not matter if it were another day. However, all of a sudden, they are the things that are stressing you up, and you feel that strong urge of screaming in rage taking over your whole body and a choking feeling as though you have swallowed a whole raw potato!

Apart from the emotional turmoil that anger brings, the sad thing with avoiding anger management sessions is the fact that it allows anger to creep in slowly and soon it may be excessive. This excessive anger is the reason why people's physical and emotional health is adversely affected by frequent complains of body pains, headaches, intense migraines and high blood pressure among other effects.

The anger outbursts that you experience spinning out of control may not just affect you but also the people around you. Your friends, workmates, and family will hurt a lot seeing you in a state of rage. You may even beat them directly when you are angry, and you act violently and aggressively. It is one of the factors that have contributed to the rampant cases of domestic violence among partners and trust me; you do not want to be one of them.

When you fail to seek help through anger management programme, specialists and other ways possible to calm your anger, you may end up hating yourself. It is that anger that is burning within you that can contribute to depression and feeling as though you are not worthy. In fact, according to studies, passion can lead you to adopt suicidal behaviors.

Therefore, having said all these, one thing that you have to bear in mind is that anger is not just another emotion that you sweep under the carpet! You have to realize that anger issues are real and the only way in which

Introduction

Anger has a close relationship with the mind. You can never change or avoid what gets into your mind through the spoken words, but you can change your reaction. You don't have to be wild and angry at everyone who makes irritates you. This is where mental training is vital. There are high chances that people who have anger management problems are aware. The problem arises in how to deal with anger when it arises.

Psychologists such as Deffenbacher Jerry, argue that some individuals have a higher chance of getting angry than others, due to the mind. Moreover, some may show their anger while others prefer to hold it in. Those who fail to release their anger openly often get grumpy and disturbed. It is further argued that people who are prone to getting angry, rarely throw stuff around and curse. Instead, they can withdraw themselves from the crowd and in some cases get sick. However, for those who hardly get angry, their reaction can be devastating if not handled properly. You may assume that someone is always calm, only to find out that they are extremely wild when angry. Sometimes, you don't even see it coming and can assume.

A low tolerance for anger is something common in individuals who don't get angry quite often. In the case that it happens, finally, they get worked up. Especially if a situation is unjust to such people, the case becomes worse. For example, when they are questioned for a meagre mistake that holds no water. Such persons are usually like this either due to psychological or genetical issues. Evidence-based research has shown that some kids are born with anger disorders. This is easily noticed through their reaction to life's issues and high rate of irritability.

The fact that many people are taught, from an early age, that anger is negative, makes it even worse to handle. Apparently, all other emotions are okay except anger, according to some people. This is a tired narrative that often creates more problems. Someone's background also has a significant role to play in their life in terms of anger and the mind.

Chapter 1. Identifying Triggers

You're having a friendly conversation with someone. Everything is going just fine, and then all of a sudden - BAM! Your heart is beating fast, your blood pressure is rising, and you're starting to feel the urge to hit the person you're talking to. What just happened was that you got triggered. Emotionally triggered, to be more accurate. But what are emotional triggers? To put it simply, emotional triggers are either people, words, objects, situations, or even smell that seems to arouse a very intense emotional reaction within a person.

Depending on the situation, an emotional might provoke feelings of rage and anger, or sometimes sadness and fear. When it comes to emotional triggers, the list is unlimited since virtually anything can trigger a person, depending on their values, beliefs, and life experience. There are three major reasons that we get triggered.

Opposing Beliefs

Beliefs give us human beings a sense of comfort and safety. They can make us do the impossible and are very powerful forces that can affect the way we live our lives. One of the reasons we get triggered is when our personal beliefs are challenged, whether intentionally or unintentionally. Our beliefs are what give birth to our values. When we feel that our beliefs are being challenged, we feel at the same time that our value system is being threatened and that we could be in danger. We get triggered when people disagree with our beliefs and values, because to us, it's like they are questioning the truth of the very thing we hold dear.

Emotional Trauma

Trauma plays a major role in the way we respond to triggers. In fact, the very expression "getting triggered" is one that's associated with PTSD or post-traumatic stress disorder that's very common among war survivors, whether soldier or civilian. Soldiers who have just returned from war, for instance, may be triggered when they hear loud noises. A girl who has been abused for a long time may be triggered when she encounters a person who looks just like her perpetrator. In the same manner, a man who had been abused by his alcoholic father as a young boy may be triggered whenever he sees a drunk man or people drinking alcohol.

Ego Preservation

In psychology, the ego is the sense of self. It's the component of an individual's personality that deals with reality and is composed of memories, thoughts, values, and beliefs. Every human being has an ego, and its aim is to protect the self through the establishment of ideals, beliefs, and habits. When the ego is challenged, the result is almost immediately the self being triggered, and more often than not, this results in us defending ourselves through arguing, insulting, defaming, sabotaging, or in extreme cases, murdering those who have hurt our ego.

Are You Being Triggered?

The thing about being triggered is that it is always accompanied by both internal and internal and external symptoms. In most cases, it causes your heart to raise and your body to tremble. It also produces hot flushes, and sometimes that feeling that you can't breathe or swallow. For some people, being triggered means having chills, feeling nauseated, sweating real hard, and sometimes even fainting.

It doesn't stop there, though. A few moments after you feel all those symptoms, almost always, the result is you feeling intense emotions of either anger, hatred, or disgust. Sometimes, if it's not anger you feel, it's fear, terror, or grief. And all these usually results in self-protective behavior that causes you to shout in anger, argue incessantly, insult the people involved, cry, or sometimes flee from the scene.

How To Identify Your Triggers

Identifying triggers is one of the first steps in anger management. When you're not aware of what triggers your anger and how to handle them, your life will be miserable. On the other hand, being able to identify your triggers successfully can provide you with a better sense of control, as well as help improve your interpersonal functioning.

Knowing how to identify your emotional triggers is very critical because if the things that provoke extreme responses from you are not brought to consciousness, you will remain hostage to your own emotions, manipulated like a puppet and not knowing what to do. Your relationships will all be ruined if not strained, your career will be sabotaged, and your life will be very miserable if you are not set free from such ignorance.

When it comes to exploring your emotional triggers, the hardest part is not the one where you identify your triggers. The hardest part is usually committing to the process. Putting in the much-needed effort in discovering your triggers is all worth it, though. The following are straightforward ways to pinpoint your hot buttons.

Be Aware Of Your Physical Reactions

The first step to identifying triggers is paying attention to your bodily reactions. Is your heart beating faster? Are you having hot or cold flushes? What's the first thing you were doing? Were you clenching your fists? Did your breathing started to speed up? It's important to take note of these details and write them down on your journal. Some physical reactions can be extreme, but others can be very subtle, so it's crucial that you don't ignore any sign no matter how insignificant it may seem at the moment.

Be Conscious Of Your Thoughts

A person's thoughts can go extreme when they're angry. Be conscious of the things firing inside your head and watch out for polarized viewpoints. In any argument, most people prefer clear positions, where they are 'right' or 'good' and the other person is 'wrong' or 'bad'. Be aware of such behavior and the thoughts running in your head but avoid doing anything to react to them. Ask yourself then what kind of stories you're creating in your mind about the situation, or the person involved and then list those things down in your journal.

Ask Yourself What Specifically Triggered Your Emotion

Once you are already aware of your bodily reactions and the thoughts going through your mind, try to identify next what or who has possibly triggered such response from you. In some cases, it could be what another person has said, or it could be an object, or maybe even a smell or aroma that triggered you. At other times, it could be that you have been triggered by another person's opinion or believe about something that's the total opposite of what you believe in. It could also be a combination of triggers, so make sure you remain vigilant. And as always, remember to write down whatever trigger you have identified. This will help you become more aware of yourself, so you can respond more ppropriately in the future.

Remember What Happened Before You Were Triggered

Your triggers can also have their own "triggers," and it's important that you are able to recognize them if you are to learn how to manage your anger. There are times that you are more susceptible to triggers and that's because something has happened before the event you were triggered. It could be that work has been extra stressful, or that you're not feeling well, or you've been dealing with difficult people all day long. Oftentimes, learning how to identify these prerequisites can help you keep yourself from being triggered by taking some precautions, such as taking a deep breath and relaxing or avoiding the situation altogether.

Identify What Needs You Have That May Have Not Been Met

Being triggered emotionally almost always means that there's some deepest need or desire of yours that have not been met. Also sometimes, when we explode in anger in front of a person, it's not because we are angry with that person, but because someone whom we expect is going to meet our need didn't.

Take the story of a young man who suddenly got mad while shopping with a friend. His friend was asking him to hurry up as they're going to be late, and all of a sudden, his facial expression changed and he suddenly became irritable. A few days later, when asked by his friend why he got angry out of nowhere, he replied that before they went shopping, he was asking to meet with his dad whom he hadn't seen for quite some time. For some reason, they weren't able to meet, which left the young man feeling ignored and unimportant.

When you're emotionally triggered, ask yourself what needs you have are being threatened or not met. Is it your need for attention? Is it your need for safety? Once you've identified those needs, list them down and reflect on what needs keep on appearing.

What To Do When You're Triggered

Recognize That You're Having a Reaction

Awareness is a key factor in managing emotional triggers. When you're being triggered, you can expect your rate of breathing to increase, as well feel your muscles begin to tense and constrict. As soon as you recognize these signs, ask yourself immediately what you're feeling and why. Stick to simply identifying your feelings; don't fear whatever emotions you have, and don't judge yourself for having such emotions.

Focus on Your Breathing

Breathing is an excellent way to relax. When you're being triggered and you choose to take a deep breath, you take your focus off whatever is irritating you. This helps you de-escalate and calm down. Deep breathing isn't simply a form of distraction, though. According to clinical psychologist Mitch Abrams, Psy.D., taking a deep breath when you're pissed helps reverse whatever is happening inside your body as a result of anger. The next time you feel you're being triggered, take a slow, deliberate, and controlled breathing. This will help shift your focus from whatever angered you, as well as help your body return to a normal, more relaxed state.

Remove Yourself from the Situation

There are times when pure deep breathing is not enough to calm you down. When you notice your relaxation techniques aren't working, do yourself a favor and take a break, removing yourself from the situation. If you're in a meeting, excuse yourself and inform everyone that you need to take a quick break. Taking a walk for a few minutes could help. As much as possible, spend this time alone. There's a higher chance for your breathing exercise to work and calm you down when you can go someplace all by yourself like a garden or the park perhaps. Only return if it's really necessary and when you've already completely calmed down.

Ask Yourself Why You're Triggered

An emotion as strong as anger has a way of blinding people. To keep yourself from being able to make the right judgments, be inquisitive and ask yourself why you're currently feeling what you're feeling. Understanding why you feel emotionally triggered will help you regain your calmness and be in control of the situation again. Most importantly, the quicker you realize that you are being triggered, the sooner you will find out whether or not the threat you perceive is real.

Postpone your Reaction

Delaying your reaction to something that triggers you may not be the answer, but it's a good way for you to get to the root of what's causing the problem as soon as possible. The idea is not to bury or control your feelings, but consciously setting them aside until you can find a way to unleash them later on in a more appropriate and healthier way. For instance, instead of exploding right in front of the person who has triggered you, you can postpone your reaction and maybe shout inside your room later on when you're all alone. That said, it's important to be careful not to suppress your anger. There's a very thin line between consciously postponing your reaction and unconsciously suppressing your emotions, which is why it's very important to learn how to improve your self-awareness.

Chapter 2. Signs and symptoms of anger and the chronic anger

Everyone feels anger. It is a normal human emotion that motivates a person to act in response to an attack, affront, or wrongdoing. It is our body's natural defense mechanism that gives us the tools to fight back, speak out, and stand up against injustice. When we get angry, the body experiences an increase in noradrenaline, hormones, and adrenaline levels. With these powerful substances rushing through our veins, the body is filled with the energy and strength needed to handle a perceived threat. A surge of hormones on their own are enough to mess with our emotions but when fueled by two powerful natural stimulants, your body and mind become a primed self-defense weapon. That is why the instinctive way to express one's anger is usually through some form of aggressive behavior as the body kicks into a fight or flight mode.

There is a difference between losing your cool once in a while and not being able to keep your anger under control. The first step to finding out if your loved one, family member, friend, or you have anger management issues, is to know the signs. There are a few key indicators that could shine a light on whether you or someone close to you may have an anger management problem.

Quick to Anger

We can all get snappy from time to time. This is especially true if you are living a high-stress life or going through something that is emotionally draining. It is your body's way of letting you know you are on the brink of an abyss that leads to some sort of a breakdown. More often than not, in cases like these, as soon as the stress and pressure are removed your temper evens out and you are back to normal. The problem comes in when you find yourself losing your temper a lot more and with each episode, your anger threshold seems to have diminished a bit more. You feel like you are in a constant bad mood and every tiny little thing makes you angry for seemingly no reason at all.

Unable to Maintain a Healthy Relationship

In a relationship, anger expresses itself in many different forms and no matter how much you love someone, there is only so much abuse a person can take. Anger can present itself as fear of expressing one's feelings in a relationship which leads to self-doubt, feelings of not being good enough, mistrust, or being incredibly shy. Fear is probably one of the most flammable anger accelerants when navigating a relationship. It can also make a person lash out in the ugliest ways, such as verbal or physical abuse, jealousy, and mistrust. Once anger takes hold inside a relationship, and is left unchecked, it tends to leave nothing but hurt and destruction in its wake. No one can maintain a healthy relationship with anyone in their life when they are suffering from unchecked anger management issues.

Self-Harm to Vent Anger and or Frustration

Hitting a wall or digging your nails into your palms to inflict pain in order to vent anger is not a healthy coping method neither does it mean you have gained control. Not only can it lead to serious injuries, infection or more fatal outcomes but it could lead or may be an indication of more serious mental health issues. Anger is often a symptom of low self-esteem, an eating disorder, depression, anxiety, bipolar disorder and substance abuse to name but a few. It could also be a sign of abuse, grief or something in your life you never quite got over or blame yourself for.

Explosive Behavior During Arguments

People, who become argumentative, throw temper tantrums, get into verbal or fist fights and have to fling things may have a problem with explosive behavior. There is a disorder called IED (Intermittent explosive disorder) where a person has violent outbursts that come on without warning and disappear nearly as fast. Their episodes may seem as if they are completely overreacting to a situation and have little to no impulse control as what was a minor infraction gets blown up into a major one. After each outburst, they will exhibit feelings of remorse, guilt, and embarrassment over the way they acted. Most people who suffer from IED usually have some underlying disorder, may have had a brain injury or it could be hereditary.

Problems Trusting People

Trust is something that does not come easy to a lot of people, especially those suffering from anger management issues. Often anger is driven by jealousy which in turn can feed a person's paranoia resulting in mistrust. Most people who suffer from anger issues tend to feel that they cannot trust those close to them or anyone at all really. They can become rather overbearing, start to question everything, become obsessive, stop believing what they are being told and may even stalk the person they do not trust. Mostly they need confirmation that their mistrust is warranted as they need someone else to blame for the burning anger driving them. It is a lot easier to be able to accuse someone of being a liar or cheat than to admit that the problem may lie within them.

Rage Blackouts

A rage black our is when a person experiences fury to the point where they black out from rage then go on a rampage tearing up anything or anyone in their way. During the blackout, they are in a dissociated state and suffer from amnesia as they perform almost superhuman feats. These blackouts usually only last no more than a few seconds to a few minutes but in that time, they can cause a lot of damage. Powered up by the body's own natural nervous system and neural stimulants they are capable of doing things that if not so terrifying would be quite amazing. Some characterize it as "going berserk" which is a term that relates back to the Norse Berserker that was said to get into such a state that would gain almost superhuman strength. This gave them the ability to forge forward in battle destroying all in their path. Foaming at the mouth and displaying fits of pure rage their own side would stay well out of their way or as far behind them as possible as the Berker could not distinguish between a friend and foe. People who suffer from rage blackouts have no control and no memory of doing the devastation they wrought until they come out of their disassociated state. The Incredible Hulk is a prime example of what a disassociated rage blackout state is like. When Dr. Banner becomes threatened or stressed his entire being is not transformed into a powerful destructive monster that he has no control of nor does he have any memories of what the Hulk does.

Loss of Control

Anger is powerful tools that can make a person feel they are back in control of what they perceive to be a threat. It is sometimes seen as a heroic act when a person takes on a situation in defense of something or someone. It can also be used to cover up feelings of fear, anxiety, and stress allowing the person to feel like they have regained some control over the situation. Although a person is completely conscious of what they are doing they are powerless to stop it as the anger feeds off the underlying issues driving them to spew out their angry tirade. While a rage blackout can be terrifying a person, who has given control over to the anger can be even more so. As they tend to home in on their target completely aware of the harm they are inflicting with deadly accuracy.

Chapter 3. How Anger Can Damage People Around You

When anger is at appropriate levels, it can spur action and responsibility for problems with a need to take care of situations in the right way. However, when it is not controlled, it can cause severe outcomes to an individual and the people around.

The first effect of anger is on you, even before it affects others. It can easily ruin your health and change how you live your life. For starters, it increases your level of stress and makes you tense even over little situations. Besides, you are more susceptible to diseases such as high blood pressure, insomnia, cardiovascular disorders, and diabetes.

When you have excessive anger, it becomes chronic, and this leads to damaged mental energy and impaired judgment. This is why people with anger disorders tend to have outbursts that make them irrational in choices and decisions. The action taken by an angry person is more likely to be biased and can harm the people around. In terms of a person's mental health, anger is poised to causing migraines, stroke, depression, and other psychological issues.

Anger also makes you uneasy and unable to release something that affects you, and this ends up hurting you more. When you are quick to anger, you will be prone to frequent outbursts on matters that are meager and insignificant. The problem isn't about people getting angry but is how you deal with it when it arises. It can damage the people around you through the following ways:

In your workplace

Your career can easily suffer the effects of anger if you are not careful. It can also affect those who work closely with you since they will experience most of the episodes.

As an individual in the workplace, anger can dismantle your creativity and thinking. It clouds your judgment and makes it hard for you to make informed decisions. It can also destroy the relationship you had with your colleagues as they will now view you differently. One way it destroys this relationship is through the loss of trust. A colleague who has regular ire and rage is less likely to be trusted by his or her co-workers. Nobody will be sure of what you can do and how you will behave when you are angry.

Whether anger is expressed or not, it is still harmful. For instance, when one doesn't express their anger, they might be withdrawn or hold grudges against others, which will affect workflow. Therefore, venting your ire or retracting yourself from the rest only creates havoc in your work experience and taints your reputation. Sometimes if you hold a position of leadership, it can affect the respect you receive from your staff or make them work in fear. When they are under duress, they will neither be productive nor free to air the concerns or contributions. As opposed to showing your anger, you can use other outlets to express it, which we will learn moving forward.

Ire can also make it challenging for you to accomplish your projects and tasks. Such things need your undivided concentration and attention. You may, at times, fail to meet deadlines and expectations, and this prevents you from maximizing your potential. It also makes people hesitant about working with you, whether in the same office or on the same project. You are also likely to face feelings of regret, shame, and guilt due to your previous reactions when angry. At times when you lose it, you may do things that you feel less proud of later on because deep down, you are aware that your actions were wrong.

It can also hinder your ability to have fun and relate with others freely. You will continuously feel left out and rejected by your colleagues, who are afraid of your actions when angry. And this can affect your mental health and lead to depression among other psychiatric conditions. The same way laughter is said to be contagious is the same for other emotions such as anger. When you get angry at a colleague, they are also vulnerable to getting the same negative feelings. This is because their brain will force them to get angry in defense of your actions. The least reaction from your colleagues when you're full of rage is intimidation, fear, feeling put off, and spikes of anger.

Aggressive anger, to be more precise, can lead to much more damage than passive anger. It can quickly turn physical and can lead to fatal injuries and massive destruction of property at work. Without self-control, it is a tragedy for you and your colleagues.

In your relationship

According to studies made, anger is one of the leading causes of relationship failures and break-ups. A lot of gender-based cases are reported worldwide due to anger outbursts. People get injured and hospitalized because of this emotion, and it is, therefore, essential to understand when the rain starts beating you.

Anger in a relationship arises mostly due to the failure to understand each other. It can have devastating effects on both partners if not appropriately handled. Solving differences through yells and violent behaviors only makes the situation worse than it already is. Everyone gets angry at times as this is typical for all humans. However, it is imperative to know how to deal with your anger so that it neither affects you or the next person. If you allow it to take the better part of you, you might end up hurting those whom you love. The reality is that constant lashing out on your spouse can reduce the chances of your relationship advancing.

When you are quick to anger in your relationship, your partner will fear opening up to you and will try to avoid spending time with you. Besides, anger affects relationships in the following ways:

- Creates tension. People are more likely to get tensed up when around a person who gets angry quickly. This is because they are unsure of what will happen in the next minute. Will you suddenly shout and yell or break something due to rage? This and other thoughts linger in your partner's mind.
- Causes frustrations. Most marriage counselors and relationship coaches argue that you should never go to bed, angry at your partner. That you should first land on a resolution before sleeping because failure to do this causes frustrations to mount and this is a remedy for a failed union. When either partner has a lot of frustrations inside, they will

quickly jump to conclusions and rush into decisions. They are also likely to apportion blames without any basis.
- Creates fear. As above mentioned, ire leads to fear in a relationship. It makes partners afraid to speak about their concerns in fear that they will be shut down rudely or interrupted with angry outbursts. Yelling at your partner with rage will make them fear you and be less open about what they truly feel. Whenever he or she has a problem that needs your attention, they would rather keep it to themselves than tell you.
- Reduces trust. When someone is living under pressure from you and is always afraid, they will most likely lose or reduce their trust towards you. This is due to the uncertainty of what you can do when you are agitated as you are highly unpredictable.
- Causes a void between people. The more your partner hesitates to talk to you or creates fear when around you, the more distant they become. This gap between people affects their relationship and can lead to extramarital affairs for couples.
- Leads to resentment. Constant ire to your significant other can lead to bottling up of feelings or emotions, which leads to resentment. This can easily add a wedge in relationships and affect how people relate. As opposed to keeping your feelings to yourself, you would instead let them out responsibly.

To handle your anger correctly in your relationship is to have a sit-down and chat the way forward together in a responsible way. As a means of doing so, try and avoid touching sensitive items that may spike anger and agitation on your partner. If both of you are not in a position to meet and talk due to unavoidable circumstances, then chatting through the phone can be a significant step to use for a start as you wait for each other's anger to subside.

In your family

A family is the basic unit of society. It is said that charity begins at home, and this statement also applies to the emotions you portray to your family. Scientists say that a family is one of the main contributors to individual character growth and development. It shapes an individual into the person he or she is. As stated earlier in the text, a person's background can contribute to their character and what they turn out to be. Many people tend to behave the same way they were raised. For instance, the experience of a mother or father who shows emotional outbursts with anger will affect how the children behave when they are displeased, especially in the future as they grow up. Children are exceptionally brilliant imitators as they copy what they see from their parents. Thus, certain behaviors that they see when young can damage their lives in the sense that they will emulate in the same manner as adults.

The effects of anger in a family are also visible in the mode of interaction among the members. It affects how people relate to each other, even in the simplest or most basic things. The earliest experience of communicating with another person starts with the family. The chances are that the same way you communicate within your family is the same way you will interact with other people outside.

Generally, people are aware of it when they can't handle their anger. In essence, they feel it when they are unable to control their emotions and how they behave. The only unfortunate thing is that many assume that this is a disorder that has no remedy, which is wrong. When dealt with accordingly, anger levels can be brought down in individuals. The hopeless feeling you get about your anger condition can easily be alleviated when you know how to deal with the state. A lot more about this will make sense as you read on.

One way to deal with anger problems in your family is to visit therapists or counselors. They can help you to understand different patterns of this mental state and how it is passed from one generation to the next. Learning this can help you to know how to manage the condition in your family in case you are stuck on what to do. Although the person faced with anger problems in the family should be given priority in therapy, the others should also get counseling so that they are not affected in their future lives.

Chapter 4. Why is Being Angry Very Unhealthy?

The thing about anger – it is often very clear cut. Anger is not an emotion you can hide for all your life. At one-point, uncontrolled anger will affect you. We ask- is there an emotion that is more misunderstood than anger? Many people believe that holding in this emotion is bad for you – it only builds on the pressure to express and the moment it chooses to come out, it will do so in unexpected ways. Prolonged anger and sudden busts are unhealthy for you. This emotion is very strong and it tends to arouse the nervous system. In fact, it produces effects in the entire body. Sadly, anger eats away at your vital organs, more so the cardiovascular system. It affects your gut and hijacks the nervous system. It also affects your ability to think clearly. Besides, unattended anger tends to grow within the body.

Know the cause of your anger.

Using the anger diary, track down the events, things, and people that trigger anger. Normally, anger is a mask for our deepest fears. Therefore, look beyond the surface – what deep and hidden fears are making you angry right now.

Let go of what you cannot control.

As you look for ways to manage your anger, know that the only thing you are actually capable of changing is yourself. It is not upon you to control how other people act, but how you react to them is entirely your choice. Getting angry does not fix the situation and in fact, it will make you feel worse. If someone keeps triggering your anger, walk away from them. If walking away is not a plausible solution, brainstorm for other possibilities.

Express your feelings

As you share how you feel, be sure to use measured tones and think first. Use the right words which are not emotionally loaded. Ensure that you are communicating in a non-confrontational but firm way. State that you are angry, explain your reason and try to find a solution.

Be cautious

Expressing how you feel in a constructive and appropriate way is a good thing. However, you need to look out for dangerous situations. For instance, if you have a jealous or abusive partner, avoid sharing with him/her. Instead, vent t a friend or trusted person. You might find a solution to your problem in a way you never imagined.

Be assertive in expressing your feelings and avoid aggression

Assertiveness requires you to speak in a nonviolent yet effective way. Sometimes you may have to rehearse your answer before delivering it to the other person.

Make positive statements

You may have to internalize some positive statements which you chant to yourself when angry. These statements will serve as a reminder that you are responsible for your own behavior. Saying the statements to yourself will also buy you some time to think before acting. They protect you from knee jerk reactions. For instance, you can say- "I can take care of my needs." "The needs of other people are as important as mine." "I am capable of making good choices."

Regardless of whether you express or suppress anger, this emotion can make you ill.

Uncontrolled anger is an emotion that has adverse physical effects. When we are angry, our bodies normally release cortisol and adrenaline hormones. These are the same hormones released when we undergo stress. When these hormones are released, our pulse, blood pressure, breathing rates, and body temperature may increase, and in extreme cases, to potentially dangerous levels. The chemical and hormonal reactions taking place when we are stressed are designed to give us instant power and a boost of energy to enable the fight or flight mode. This means that the mind and body are activated to run or defend themselves from danger.

However, people with anger management issues (getting angry often) can become ill because of the unregulated physical reactions. Just like stress left unmanaged, anger too can make a person ill. Basically, our bodies do not have the capacity to handle excessive levels of cortisol and adrenaline especially if these hormones and chemicals are constantly released. Some of the problems that may occur because of regular anger occurring over long periods of time include.

- Sleep problems
- Skin disorders
- Problems with digestion,
- Aches and pains more so in the back and head,
- The reduced threshold of pain,
- High blood pressure which might lead to cardiac arrest and stroke
- Impaired immunity,
- Anger may also lead to psychological problems including.
- Depression
- Alcoholism
- Self-injury
- Substance abuse
- Eating disorders
- Reduced self-confidence

Some of the key things you should note about anger being unhealthy for you are;

- Chronic anger will increase your chances of getting a stroke or heart attack. It will also weaken your immune system.
- The best ways to deal with anger immediately include taking deep breaths and walking away.
- In the long term, anger can be managed through identifying its triggers, changing your reactions and seeking professional help.

Anger can be good when expressed in a healthy way and addressed quickly. In fact, under certain circumstances, anger can help one to think rationally. However, unhealthy anger will wreak havoc within your body and also to the people around you. When you hold anger in for long periods, it will explode into a full rage. If y have unhealthy episodes of anger or are prone to losing your anger every so often, below are some of the reasons you should learn anger management.

Anger outbursts put your heart at risk.

Research have revealed that anger outbursts affect a person's cardiac health. How so? Basically, in the first two hours after an outburst, your chances of getting a heart attack double. This research was found to be truer in men. Anger is physically damaging.

If you fail to express anger in an appropriate manner, it becomes some quiet poison in the body. Gradually, repressed anger will explode and might lead you to an early death. Researchers found that people who are more prone to anger (and that anger becomes part of their personality) are at a higher risk of coronary disease compared to those who are less angry.

To protect your ticker (heart), it is important to identify and address your emotions and more so anger before they go out of control. Basically, everything in excess is poisonous. However, it is important to note that constructive anger is not associated with heart diseases.

Constructive anger involves that which you speak directly to the person that is upsetting you and identifying a solution. It is the kind of anger that makes you more rational.

Anger increases your chances of getting a stroke.

If you have a challenge of controlling anger and you keep lashing out at people for every other thing, beware. One study revealed that people with anger management challenges are at three times higher risk of getting a stroke. How? you may ask. During the two hours following an anger outburst, there are chances of getting a blood clot in your brain and bleeding within the brain to death. For those with an aneurysm in one or more of the brain arteries, there is a six times higher chance of rupturing it after an outburst.

The good news is that one can learn how to control these explosions. First, identify your triggers, then learn how to change your responses. Instead of letting your anger control you, do some exercises, change your environment, use assertive communication skills, learn some other anger management skills to stay in charge.

Anger weakens your immune system

If you are angry all the time, you might have noticed that you get ill often. The confused state of your body that occurs when you are angry interferes with the levels of the antibody immunoglobulin A. These are the body cells' first line of defense against illnesses and anger issues lower them for at least six hours after an outburst. If you are habitually angry and keep losing control, protect your immune system through several coping strategies including effective problem solving, assertive communication, through restructuring and humor. You need to get away from the black and white mentality and be more open to the opinions of others. Remember that agreeing with the opinion of another person does not make you a loose. Letting another person have his/her way does not make you weak. Either way, you have to start staying calm for the sake of your immunity.

- Anger problems make a person anxious.

Lack of control makes you worried though you may not notice. Anger and anxiety go hand in hand. One study conducted in 2012 revealed that anger can worsen the symptoms of generalized anxiety disorder. This condition is characterized by uncontrollable and excessive worry that interrupts the normal life of a person. People with GAD were found to have higher levels of anger and also hostility. This anger was mostly internalized and unexpressed thus contributing more to the severity of the anxiety problem.

- Anger has also been linked to depression.

Anger, Aggression, and depression are connected. According to numerous studies, these three states are interconnected especially in men. Most people suffering from depression have passive anger – that is, a form of anger whereby a person ruminates about the issue at hand but hardly takes action. The biggest problem with this kind of anger is that it pulls the person deeper into the cycle of depression. Psychologists advise that when one is struggling with depression, he should get busy in order to avoid over-thinking about things.

Any activity that gets your mind off the things brewing anger is advised. Get involved in biking, golfing, painting, singing, or any other thing that draws your mind away from anger. These activities tend to fill your mind up and draw it to the present moment. There is no more room for you to brew anger once your mind is occupied by other things.

- Anger can hurt your lungs.

If you thought that smoking is the only bad practice that might hurt your lungs, here is some news. Being perpetually angry can hurt your lungs. Anger leads to hostility which in turn affects the capacity of your lungs. Research conducted by Harvard University scientists over eight years about anger and its effects found that people with chronic anger and high hostility rates had a lower lung capacity compared to others. The men with the highest hostility rating had a lower lung capacity. Consequently, they were at risk of developing some respiratory problems. The scientists theorized that an increase in stress hormones associated with feelings of anger creates inflammations in the airways.

- Anger shortens life.

As the saying goes, happy people live longer. Stress is directly connected to general health. Stress and anger interfere with your lifespan. Research conducted by the University of Michigan revealed that people who held onto anger for long have a shorter lifespan than those who express their feelings in a constructive way.

If you are a person who is uncomfortable expressing his emotions, practice how to constructively share your feelings. If working on your own does not seem to work, seek help from a therapist. A healthy expression of anger is actually very beneficial. If a person infringes on your rights you have every reason to tell them that they are wrong. Ensure that you tell people exactly how you feel and what you need in a firm yet respectful way.

Chapter 5. Positive Ways to Express Anger

When Jane happened to come across a rather suspicious text on her partner's mobile phone, she immediately suspected him of cheating on her. She confronted her partner about the same that night. It turns out, she wasn't wrong, and he indeed was cheating on her with his colleague. However, he did promise to end the affair and never indulge such behavior again. Jane was livid with anger and asked her partner to leave their house. But he started to cry, apologize, and even plead with her to not end the relationship. She finally relented and allowed him to stay. However, that night and the next couple of days, anger kept piling up within her. She did not express the anger she was expressing, continued to smile like she always did, and even tried to be nice to her partner. Over the next couple of days, the anger kept simmering within her. Stress started to build up. A part of Jane wanted to stay well behaved and exhibit socially accepted behavior and love her partner. However, another part of her, the one which was livid with anger, wanted to do anything but that. After ten days, she fell sick due to a combination of depression, fatigue, and sore throat. It isn't surprising that she fell sick. As you know, anger is a very powerful emotion, and keeping it bottled up within made her sick.

Everyone has experienced anger at one point or another in their lives. The real question is, what can you do with this feeling? Should you act on it or must you repress it? If you act on your anger, more often than not, you will end up hurting yourself or someone dear to you. On the other hand, if you keep it all bottled up within, it will increase the stress you feel. Apart from this, suppressing anger can harm your physical, mental, and emotional well-being. Well, it seems like regardless of what course of action you plan to take, anger can hurt you either way. Therefore, it is quintessential that you learn to deal with your anger constructively and express it healthily. At times, you cannot avoid your anger and, in such cases, expressing it constructively is a good idea. By doing this, you are not only acknowledging your emotions but are able to express it too.

Express Anger Without Hurting Others

Learning to express your anger constructively will reduce any stress you experience and also make you feel heard. If you want to lead a healthy and happy life, then you must learn to not only manage your anger, but you must also learn about the ways in which you can express it healthily. In this section, you will learn about creative ways that you can direct your anger toward something constructive.

It might sound a little old fashioned but writing down your feelings on paper when you are angry will help you feel better. Grab a pen and a sheet of paper and start noting everything that you are feeling. The things you write don't necessarily have to make sense. This is a great way to get rid of any undesirable thoughts. Also, once you write things down, it will give you a better understanding of why you are feeling the way you do. If you like to draw or paint, then go ahead and do so. If not, you can always purchase a coloring book and use it for therapeutic reasons. Coloring and painting will distract your mind from any angry thoughts.

Play a sport. It is never too late to learn to play a sport. Perhaps you were always interested in learning to play tennis. Well, there is no time like the present to learn. Playing a sport gives your body a chance to get rid of the anger and replace all the stress hormones with feel-good ones. You can play tennis, volleyball, basketball, or anything you like. Another great way to express your anger is by practicing. Throwing punches will certainly calm you down. Once you are calm, you can start thinking rationally. You can also go to the gym and exercise if you want. Exercising will not only help manage and express your anger constructively, but it will also improve your overall health. If none of these sports appeal to you, you can go on a run or go for a relaxing dip in the pool.

Singing can calm you down. Listening to music can be relaxing, while singing along can be a great stress buster. You can sing the way you want and don't hesitate even if you cannot sing. Use your voice to express your anger constructively. Dancing is a good way to let out your anger too. Dance to your heart's content. You can turn your living room into a dance floor and let go of your anger.

Start using a gestalt technique for verbalizing your anger. Place a chair across from you and imagine that the person you are angry with is sitting opposite to you. Start verbalizing why you are upset and what triggered you to the imaginary person. Let out your anger, and once you do this, you will feel better.

Once you do all these things, you will be able to talk calmly. You can use a combination of these techniques to calm down. When you are calm and have regained your composure, it is easier to talk about the things that bother you. The techniques discussed in this section will not only help regulate your anger but are great ways to tackle any stress you experience too.

Deal with Anger Constructively

Any issues with anger are often linked to various mental, emotional, physical, or even social challenges that one faces. In this section, you will learn about ways in which you can deal with your anger constructively.

Don't avoid any confrontation

A lot of people find anger to be an uncomfortable emotion and tend to avoid any confrontation. However, anger is a legitimate emotion and can help identify any problems you are facing. Shying away from anger or repressing it will only lead to an angry outburst in the future. Think of your mind as a pressure cooker and your anger as the steam that builds up within. If you don't let the pressure out, then the cooker will burst. It might not happen immediately, but it will eventually happen, and it cannot be avoided. If you don't want to have an unhealthy episode of anger, then you must learn to accept, embrace, and understand your anger.

It is time to get in touch with your feelings and any repressed feelings you are harboring within. Is it possible that the present situation triggered a rather uneasy memory from your past? Perspective is quite important if you want to settle a conflict and walk away unscathed. Don't write off your feelings or emotions as being silly. Learn to validate your feelings if you want to control them. A lot of people keep their anger bottled up because they don't like confrontations. However, dealing with the emotion that's troubling you is better than allowing it to trouble you for longer. You don't have to suppress your anger.

Avoid the blame game

No one likes to be told they are wrong, and no one likes being caught on the wrong side. However, if you get defensive and attack the person who pointed out your mistake, it will only worsen the situation. Learning to express your anger constructively is about communicating what you feel and the reasons for it. Don't be under any misconceptions that it is okay to put others down while expressing your anger constructively. For instance, if your loved one has let you down, don't resort to name calling or blaming them. Instead, you must concentrate on telling them about how their actions hurt you. Indulging in the blame game is never a solution, and it will not solve your issues. While talking about an issue that angered you, try to stay on the topic. Stay in the present and only talk about the things that upset you. It might be quite tempting to bring up the past or point out their flaws; however, doing all this will only worsen the situation and might even cause irreparable damage to the relationship. If you don't blame others, it becomes easier to diffuse the situation.

Keep your calm

It might seem quite tempting to have a big rant. However, understand that there are better ways in which you can get your point across to the other person. You need to stay calm if you want to express your anger constructively. Something as simple as the tone of your voice can make a huge difference while conveying your anger; the words you use matter too. When you're communicating, ensure that you are conveying to the other person that you care about them and that you don't have any harsh feelings towards them. While expressing your anger constructively, your goal must be not to hurt the other person, but it must be about trying to explain the reasons for your anger. When you stay calm and levelheaded, it becomes easier to talk about the things that are bothering you. Engaging in a confrontation is not a bad idea; however, letting your emotions control you is certainly a bad idea. When you keep your cool and talk calmly, it will prevent the situation from escalating. When you're angry, you might say things that you will regret later. Therefore, the trick is to recognize this earlier on and stop it before it gets out of hand. It might not be easy, but you need to pay attention to what you're saying and the way you say it.

For this strategy to work, if you require some thought in advance, consider all the benefits that you can get by approaching conflicts with a calm mind. It certainly will increase the chances of you being listened to, reduces the scope for any guilt later on, and it does not harm your relationship. All these things will give you the motivation to keep you calm, even in a stressful situation.

Keep things professional

If the person you're confronting isn't a family friend, your partner, family member, or as a colleague at work, then remember to keep things professional. Before you decide to confront the person, ensure that you take a couple of deep breaths and calm yourself. Please don't allow yourself to get overly emotional in the situation. Try to end the confrontation as soon as you possibly can and try to resolve the issue too. While engaging in such a confrontation, ensure that you have all the necessary facts to support your statements. Instead of blaming others, come up with suggestions on ways in which you can deal with certain circumstances in a better manner in the future.

However, just because you're angry doesn't mean that you have the liberty to allow it to spin out of control. By practicing these simple steps mentioned in this chapter, you can easily express your anger constructively.

Try Yoga

Yoga has been used for hundreds of years because of its healing properties. It helps improve your overall well-being — mental, physical, and emotional. The different poses suggested by yoga improve not only your flexibility but also have a calming effect on your body and mind. It is normal to get angry. Perhaps there have been instances wherein your anger ruined an entire day or upset your mood for days together. Anger is as important an emotion like joy, but you must learn to calm yourself and refocus so that you don't allow anger to control you. There are different practices and techniques suggested by yoga, which can help regain control of your anger.

The first step is to realize and accept the fact that you are angry. Take a couple of deep and calming breaths as soon as you experience a wave of anger. This must be your first line of defense. When you acknowledge any anger you feel, the next step is to consider the damage your anger can cause if you give into it. Once you do these two things, you can start using different yoga poses to regain your composure and reel in your anger.

Here are a couple of basic yoga poses that can help curb your anger.

The Corpse Pose or Savasana is considered to be the most relaxing of yoga poses. It helps calm you down mentally as well as physically. To perform this pose, all you have to do is lie down on the ground or the yoga mat on your back. Place your arms by your sides with your palms facing upward. Allow your feet to rest comfortably and keep breathing until it goes back to its natural state. The only thing you must concentrate on is your breathing. Concentrate on the calming effect of your breath and nothing else. Try emptying your mind of all thoughts. Once you do this for a couple of minutes, you will feel better.

The Child's Pose comes in handy while trying to strengthen the relationship between your body and mind. It is believed that this pose can help you get in touch with your true feelings. This is another pose that has been designed with the sole purpose of promoting relaxation. To assume this pose, you must assume the tabletop pose. You essentially need to get down on all fours. Slowly move your arm backward and place them by the side of your body. While doing this, slowly move your head closer to the ground until your forehead is resting on the floor. If you want, you can also stretch your arms forward and extend them until they lie on either side of your head.

Nose Breathing is one of the most effective breathing techniques prescribed by yoga. The great thing about this exercise is that you can perform it whenever and wherever you want. It is also known as the

Complete Breath or the Three-Part Breathing exercise. It helps purify your mind and get rid of any anger. Don't be in a hurry while doing this. To perform this exercise, you must start out by sitting with your back straight. Place a hand on your abdomen if you want to and let the other one rest on your thigh. Start by inhaling slowly and deeply through your nose. Let the breath that you take fill up your abdomen, and you can feel your abdomen move upward. Then, it is time to exhale slowly, and you will be able to feel the air rushing out of your body and through your nose. Repeat this exercise for a couple of minutes, and you will feel calm and refreshed.

Another simple breathing technique that you can follow is to take breathe in deeply through your nose. Breathe in deeply at the count of four: one, two, three, and four. Now, you must hold your breath to the count of four: one, two, three, and four. The third step is to slowly exhale through your mouth to the count of four: one, two, three, and four. The final step is to hold your breath to the count of four before you inhale. Repeat this exercise whenever you feel stressed or angry. It will quickly help dispel any internal tension and allow you to see things clearly.

Chapter 6. How to Control Your Anger without Drugs

A lot of people deal with anger and other issues involving extreme emotions the easy way. There I said it. Make no mistake about it taking mood-altering or mellowing drugs is the easier way to handle extreme emotions. If you easily get triggered and your emotions often get the better of you,

I really can't blame you for taking anti-anxiety medication, mood-altering legal prescription drugs or recreational drugs. A lot of people smoke marijuana because they want to mellow out. They want to chill. Without weed, their emotions often get the better of them. They're sick of it so they just self-medicate.

In fact, I know a lot of people who do this. When I was in college, one of the coolest guys I knew smoked a lot of weeds, and it was easy to see why because he can't go a few days without pot because he gets really angry. He's a very emotional person. He reacts easily to even the slightest disappointment, slightest negativity, and he always has to judge people, situations, and things. He has to always have the final word.

As you can well imagine, hanging out with such a person is what a lot of people would call "an acquired taste". He was a dear friend of mine, and what made it really easy to hang out with him was when he was stoned, which was pretty much one-third to one-half the time. He's a completely different person. He was just chill. In fact, he would be the mellowest person in the room. Everybody's just pumped up. It's easy for people to get all emotional as a group, but he would always be the anchor of sensibility and reason in a large part due to all that THC floating through his bloodstream.

Drugs are definitely one way to deal with emotional issues. As you can well imagine, it's not the optimal way. What if you have to operate heavy machinery? What if you have to drive? What if you have to be around children? Do you see the problem here?

Legal mood-altering drugs like antidepressants, anti-anxiety medications are not any better either. The side effects can be quite formidable. We're talking about sexual dysfunction, lack of appetite or increased appetite. There have been also many claims regarding suicidal thoughts.

Make no mistake about going with legal medication is not a slam dunk either. What if I told you that you can control your anger without drugs? You're probably rolling your eyes, you're probably even laughing out loud but it's absolutely true. You don't have to mellow out with medication.

Here's an overview. You need to go through the following steps. If you go through these the correct way, you will be able to get out from under your anger. I know this all seems too good to be true at this stage. You're probably reeling from the tremendous force of your anger. It's like almost irresistible.

I understand that but let me tell you if you do these steps and you follow everything correctly, it will improve your ability to manage your anger. In fact, you would be able to control it to the point where your life can become so much better, and the best part to all of this is that it doesn't involve any kind of self-deception, electric shock, mind-altering drugs or any extreme measures.

Instead, it all involves you taking more active control over your thought patterns. A lot of people have a tough time with this because this requires effort, attention, and energy. The good news here is you don't have to be a hero. You don't have to achieve miraculous results right out of the gate. By simply trying over and over again in simple steps, eventually, you will get there. What's important is consistency.

I'm not expecting you to master all these steps the first time around. It's usually a better idea to stick to one step and keep practicing it until you master it. Once you are comfortable with that step, and it happens naturally for you, you can go on to the next step. Master that and then you move on.

Don't think for a second that you have to race through this. There is no race to run here. You're not competing against anybody else. Just because you're going through this at a pace that you think is too slow doesn't mean that there's something wrong with you.

We're all different people. We're wired differently. We have different experiences. Accordingly, we go through new materials based on our own personal speed.

Given that you are essentially dealing with your emotions and how you process the stimuli that you pick out from the rest of the world, you are entitled to your pace. Nobody can call you out for being slow. Nobody can hold you to some sort of timeline. I need to make this clear, so you don't put any unnecessary pressure on yourself. Again, this is not a race.

Even if you take baby steps forward, that's still good news. How come? Baby steps forward are still stepping forward. You're still headed in the right direction.

Chapter 7. Communication and Anger Management

There are different types of communication styles applied by people. Angry people usually take certain postures and communication stances when they communicate with other people. In psychology, there are terms used to describe these communication stances, each taking on its own motto:

1. Aggressive communication - In this posture, the person says, "I am worthy but you are not."

2. Passive communication - The person using this posture normally says, "I don't count."

3. The passive aggressive communication - In this posture, a person says "I am worthy. You are not worthy, but I will not tell you."

4. Assertive communication – the people in this posture say that "I am worthy, and so are you."

It is evident that most angry people use more passive aggressive and aggressive postures. The people that use aggressive posture have higher chances of starting an argument; therefore, failing to reach the goal they intended to pursue. Being passive in communication is also bad in communication because it gives off the aura of weakness therefore inviting further aggression. Assertive communication is more useful and balanced since it takes into account the feelings of all the parties in the picture. It is the only posture that communicates respect for everyone. Assertive communication is most probably the best way of ensuring that every person has their needs accounted for. It is therefore very imperative that one learns how to communicate assertively rather than aggressively or passive-aggressively in order to pass and constructively receive messages.

People who have a habit of being aggressive tend to misinterpret the meaning of being assertive. To be specific, these people tend to confuse aggression and assertiveness. They think that their actions and words are assertive. The two communication styles can involve persuasion and fierce communication. However, there are fundamental things that differ for instance; the aggressive communicators tend to take the defensive while the assertive people stand up for their rights and themselves without crossing the lines of others. Typically, aggressive communication will berate and attack others regardless of the situation. On the other hand, assertive communication will only use anger and fierceness when defending. Assertive communication does not cross the lines of others unnecessarily.

Request Making and Anger Management

The style of communication that one uses determines the ability of a person to make requests. Normally, people who use aggressive communication technique have challenges making requests in an effective manner. Remember that angry people normally use aggressive communication; therefore, will fail at making requests. Because they already feel entitled, the angry people make a wrongful assumption that every person should do their bidding. They, therefore, will not make requests under the assumption that the people around them know when to make requests and how to make them. Even when they try to make requests, they make them in a way that it sounds like a demand, which then provokes anger in others and will not happily carry out the request. An effective request should involve clarity, emotional transparency and respectfulness.

Clarity refers to the making of a well-formed request which states clearly the wants and needs of the individual. When a request lacks clarity, it becomes hard to fulfill and will most probably lead to anger, frustration, and stress. This is more so the case when requests are put forward and interpreted as commands. A clear request needs to be stated explicitly and must give clear answers to certain questions that is, who, what and when.

Emotional transparency involves stating the real feelings instead of making accusations. For instance, if one tells the other "You idiot, you are so insensitive. What is it with you that you must always forget? Where is the milk, I told you to buy? Can't you even remember such small things?" Can you feel the intensity of the defense in the statement? The person is avoiding stating the real feelings and accusing the other of being an idiot. Such a request will turn a sympathetic crowd off very fast. The request lacks emotional transparency, therefore failing to appeal to the other person. Emotional transparency involves the willingness to share real feelings. The speaker sounds rude and self-centered. But if we pay closer attention to the feelings, we will sense that the speaker feels left out or neglected.

It will be better if one states his/her requests with emotional transparency, sharing the real reason for the request. That transparency is likely to motivate the listener into acting. In the example given above, we can rephrase "I feel like to do not care about me when you forget to pick something for me. Please remember to keep it for me next time." In this phrase, the speaker makes it clear that his/her feelings are hurt when the other person forgets to deliver as requested. This result in two good things, first, the message is clear, and secondly, it leaves no room for the listener to take a defensive stand. When requests are made with emotional transparency, clarity, and respect, there are high chances that the listener will take it to heart.

Respectfulness involves forming the request in a manner that makes the person want to comply. Respect makes people feel honored therefore are more likely to comply with the person making the request. When making requests, statements such as 'if it is not too much to ask, could you please....', "would you please help me....", or "I would really appreciate if you...."

There is a good request formula that helps one to pass information clearly called the Assertive Request Formula. This formula involves three parts that add up to one complete statement:

"I feel....when you.....because ...."

It is, however, very important that one makes sure that he/she does not accuse the other when making the request. For instance, one should not say "I feel that you are silly." The 'I feel section' is about how you feel. The formula does not work on accusations. This is because you will have made an accusation and made the other person to take a defensive stance based on the aggressive attacking statement. Talk about yourself in order to get better results. For instance, you can say "I feel deserted when you fail to call me and let me know that you will be late because I get worried that you might be in danger."

Chapter 8. How to Deal with Stress to Get Rid of Anger

Run the Stress Off

Running is a great way of combating stress. It is one of the easiest and beneficial physical exercises anyone can engage in. If you are feeling beat down by the rigors of life, take a run down your street of get to the nearest field and run a few laps. There are several benefits that you will experience if you run regularly:

- Running being an aerobic exercise- increases the heart rate and makes you sweat, stimulates the release of endorphins which are the body's natural feel-good chemicals, leaving your brain elated and making you happy.

- You will shed calories which will help with lowering your blood pressure and keeping your arteries in good shape.

- Running slows the aging process and reduces bone and muscles loss by building strength and flexibility. It keeps you active and improves your overall health.

- When running, you have all the time to yourself which allows you to process your thoughts. You may use the time to aid you with sorting out some issues that you may be facing or to think through a problem.

- Researchers have found out that people who are regular runners lead a happier more stress free life and are generally fitter than those who do not. Your concentration and alertness is also enhanced.

Now, put on those running shoes and hit the road for a healthier, happier and stress free life. Running can be done almost anywhere you go, you do not have to worry about where to perform this exercise. It is recommended that you drink a lot of water if you are a runner, drink at least a liter of water an hour to two hours before your run. This helps with hydration of the body, and you are unlikely to suffer dehydration.

You will not regret your decision as the benefits that will accrue to you are many.

Take a Hike

Hiking is a relaxing walk through a natural surrounding usually at a nature trail, a park or a forest. Much like running, hiking is a great exercise for stress relief though less vigorous. Hiking combines the benefits of an effective aerobic exercise, natural serene surrounding and the chance and time to relax and think freely.

The following are ways by which hiking helps the body to deal with stress:

Mental relaxation

Hiking provides the time and opportunity for mind relaxation by getting you up close to nature. Nature has been proven as a catalyst to mental relaxation by giving you the experience and wonders of natural surroundings.

Energizing the Body

Hiking being an aerobic exercise invigorates the body and helps with the regulation of stress chemicals. People who hike regularly have higher levels of feel good hormones like endorphins which reduce stress considerably.

Emotional wellbeing

When you are stressed, you are a prisoner of negative emotions like sadness, anger, nervousness etc. Hiking will activate positive energy in your body which will in turn boost your emotions to make you feel better and happier.

Brain exercising

A hike will afford you the silence and time to think profoundly about things that are important to you. Aerobic exercise coupled with deep thinking will effectively enhance the body's stress management capabilities.

Spiritual nourishment

Being in a natural environment with the wonderful serenity offers the body a chance to get spiritually fulfilled. Your nerves will be calmed, and you will get the opportunity for mental clarity and relaxation that you would normally not have every day. Hiking is a great exercise for anger and stress relief, and you ought to prepare in advance before you go on a hike. Pack a first aid kit, drinking water and a phone in case you may be confronted with an accident.

Come on, why don't you start hiking for a change? It may just be the answer to dealing with the stress you have been under lately. So, book an appointment with nature for exercise, mental and spiritual fulfillment and say goodbye to stress and anger.

Pedal the Stress Away

Do you remember how happy you were riding your bicycle when you were young? I remember my experience and I could give anything to feel the same way again. Exciting, happy and a sense of unbridled freedom. It was just a great time without a care in the world. Well, you do not have to look back to your childhood with such nostalgia because you can readily bring back those feel good moments you had on your bicycle then to the present to replace all the anger and worries you are facing now!

Don't you want to?

Cycling is another form of aerobic exercise which is great for stress relief, fitness and general well-being. When you are overwhelmed by life's pressures simply hop on a bike and start pedaling for stress relief. Being on the bike will take your mind off the problems that are bothering you, pump some feel good chemicals into your blood stream, pace you heart to leave you feeling refreshed and emotionally elated.

You can cycle after work, on weekends or your day off or even to work and while doing this, employ the meditative technique of mantra by chanting a positive phrase or word to the rhythm of your pedaling. I assure you that you will be surprised at how fats your mind will be cleared of the negativity and stress that you are facing.

Cycling is not an expensive endeavor; just buy a bicycle and you may start. It is not a vigorous if done for leisure or exercise and can be taken up by people of all ages. Cycling will keep you fit, work out your heart for better health and emotional balance. It helps with the management of chronic conditions like diabetes, cardiovascular problems and high blood pressure. The healthier and better you feel the less likely you are to be stressed. Get on your bike and enjoy the stress relieving benefits you have been missing.

Reading for Stress Relief

Reading is cathartic and is a great reliever of stress for people who are facing everyday pressures and adversity by relaxing the brain and managing the thought process. When you read your mind travels away from the pressures you are facing. You sink into the story where you will find yourself in faraway worlds. In the duration of your reading, you shall be transported away from your troubles, and this helps in balancing your emotional wellbeing.

Reading is a great mental exercise which stimulates brain activity thereby improving mental concentration and alertness. Stress fighting chemicals that give you a happy feeling are released into the brain. An active mind is strong and more likely to cope with daily pressures. You will also fight stress from the motivation and hope you derive from reading biographies and motivational books. Books and other literature are sources of information which enables you to learn more and aid in problems solving.

A book will divert your thoughts from the lingering problems or worries that are stressing you out. Set aside a few hours in your day to read and you will experience how fulfilling it can be in your efforts at dealing with stress.

When you clear your mind of negativity even for a few hours, you will make huge strides in mental relaxation. With a relaxed mind you should be able to be more creative and relaxed enabling you to cope with stress. An active mind also slows down the aging process leaving you feeling younger physically and mentally. A strong healthy body is less prone to stress.

If the last time you read was for an exam or for a school assignment, make a hot cup of tea, make yourself comfortable on your favorite seat and immerse yourself into a book. The benefits for your life and health are great, you need to try it. Get literature that appeals to you, a book, magazine or newspaper and make it a habit to read regularly for a less stress life every day.

Be a Positive Thinker

Have you heard of positive thinking? Well, the world works in a very simple way in that whatever you think is what will be manifested in your life. You attract what you think! It may seem simplistic or difficult to accept but take the time to mull it over and you realize that it is true. If you want to get that new job you applied to or want to get promoted, it begins by you wanting it then believing that you can get it without having a shred of doubt.

Self-belief is a powerful stress reliever. To always be positive and to be ever optimistic. The power of positive thinking is incredible. If you look forward to good things you will have a happier, less stressful life. Positive thinking is a state where you look forward to favorable outcomes in whatever you do. Positive thinking therefore involves actively training your mind to have creative thoughts that transform energy into reality.

Avoid dwelling on your failures and concentrate on the successes, use the disappointments as lessons for the future. Studies show that positive thinking leads to a longer and healthier life since you are less prone to stress. You become a positive thinker by identifying the negative aspects of your thinking and avoid them while constantly evaluation your thoughts to make sure you stay on the positive.

Do not be too hard on yourself, allow yourself joyous moments and take time to have fun. Surround yourself with like-minded people who will help you build the habit of positive thinking. When you are optimistic you become less critical and are instead more creative and hopeful. An optimistic mindset is able to deal with stress at work more easily and constructively. Positive thinking is a powerful tool in fighting stress and anger. Try it and you are sure of great benefits and a happy relaxed life.

Time Management

If you are always late and short of time, then you are most likely leading a stressed and anxious life. There is nothing as stressful as the struggle to always meet a deadline or catch up with something you forgot about. Using the little time, we have properly will help you cope with stress. Time management involves methods aimed at using time efficiently to perform all the tasks we have within a given time and involves prioritizing, scheduling and organizing.

You must assess the tasks on your plate and put them in order of importance and urgency to avoid confusion, conflicts and unnecessary time pressures. Plan things in advance to avoid last minute scrambling in an effort get something that skipped your mind done. Good time management makes you a more productive person. You will do more within a short time thus gaining more control of your life.

Create a schedule and stick to it. You will have enough free time to engage in fun things that you have been missing. You will have time to go to the movies, play a game or any other fun activity which serves to boost health and wellbeing. Good time management means that you have enough time for work, family and friends. These moments with loved ones are most fulfilling and stress relieving.

It does not take much to be a good time manager. All you need is to start and commit to it. Well managed time leads to a more comfortable and happy life. Benefits of time management for a less stressful life are:

- Doing more with less time.
- Getting more free time which allows time to relax.
- Stress is reduced since you do not worry about pending deadlines etc.
- Higher productivity since you are fresh mentally, physically and highly motivated.

Time management is good because you will be happier, more successful, more productive, live a fuller and stress-free life. Why don't you start managing your time better and enjoy the benefits?

Get Enough Sleep

Are you sleeping enough? Lack of adequate sleep is a big contributor to incidences of stress and anger. Getting sufficient sleep is essential in your effort to deal with stress. During sleep your body gets the chance to rest, to heal and to be rejuvenated. When you do not get enough sleep, you are left susceptible to stress and other health problems because you are emotionally imbalanced.

Therefore, it is imperative to have a sleeping schedule and follow it so that you condition your body into a routine for sufficient rest. In fact, sleep deficiency is a great source of stress and anger since you are tired, irritable and have weakened creativity. Between work and your personal affairs, you probably end up not getting enough sleep. It is recommended that you sleep for at least six hours for optimal rest. However, many of us do not meet this target as studies show that most of us sleep for as little as two hours and a maximum of four hours in a 24-hour cycle!

We do not get sufficient sleep because of our poor bedtime habits that end up interfering with our sleep. To sleep better and longer, try the following:

- Set a sleeping schedule. You will sleep better if your bedtime is predictable. Your body will adapt, and you will rest more.
- Do not indulge in a heavy meal during dinner. Have a light meal at least two hours before you retire to bed.
- Physical exercise is a great sleep inducer. Work out three to four hours before you sleep.
- Do not take caffeinated drinks close to your bedtime. Your last caffeine drink should be averagely six hours or more before you lay down.
- Keep away from alcohol four to six hours before your bedtime. It will disrupt your sleep.

Sleep well for emotional balance. You will wake up refreshed, well rested and energized. When your body has this balance, it can easily manage or ward off stress.

Listening To Soothing Music

Music is very relaxing and has the ability to change moods positively by acting on our minds to avert stress. It acts quickly, is available and will relieve you of stress and anger. The calming effect of music has a distinctive relationship to our emotions and is an effective way to cope with stress. Slow classical music is extremely peaceful and has positive effect on our bodies and minds. This kind of music has its advantages. It slows the heart and pulse rates, reduces the production of stress hormones and blood pressure.

Music engrosses our thoughts to distract us from whatever worries may be lingering in our minds. Most times when you are stressed and anxious, your mind tends to wander off causing you to think of the things that cause you more anger. However, music acts as a cushion and helps your mind to relax and better concentrate.

For years music has been proven to treat ailments and restore coherence and balance between your body and mind. Furthermore, research has it that music is therapeutic in the following ways:

- Some music compositions can help disabled people by boosting harmonization and communication and improve their life.

- The use of headphones when listening to music can lessen anger and stress especially when one is about to go for surgery and after the surgery.

- During extreme pain or post-surgery, music has been known to ease and numb the pain.

- Music is also known to alleviate depression and enhance self-esteem in older people.

- Music is food for the soul. The next time you are facing adversity or are feeling down from mental fatigue or some other worries, turn on your favorite music. Enjoy the relaxing and positive vibes that will be provided by the music.

Share your problems by Talking to Someone

A problem shared is a problem solved or half solved. How insightful this is. Sharing our problems is therapeutic and a quick fix to stress. Putting a lid on your suffering and keeping it to yourself is an emotional burden and is very unhealthy. Many of us are fiercely independent and would want to solve our problems on our own. However, there is a point where you are better off talking to someone about what you are going through.

Pent up emotions and suffering will turn you into a very stressed and imbalanced person. Reach out to someone you trust- a friend or relative for a listening ear and realize the great positive impact it will have on you. Talking to someone has the following benefits:

- Sharing your problems will help you get rid of bad emotions like worries, anger etc. You will feel better after since you will have let go of the emotional burden.
- Your pain is reduced since you will have someone sharing your problem and empathizing with you.
- Solutions to your problems are easier to come by as you will be readily advised by the listener.
- By sharing you lead a healthier life since you negate the effects of emotional distress caused by pent up emotional turmoil.
- You will simply feel better and happier at having talked about whatever is bothering you.

By sharing we get the load off our chests leaving us emotionally boosted, relaxed and stronger. It also prevents the situation from deteriorating to a much deeper problem like depression or emotional breakdown. With a relaxed and more stable mental state, you have the clarity and strength to handle your problem and will easily embark on problem solving for a stress-free life.

From now on if you find yourself in a tight place emotionally and are feeling stressed, seek someone you can share your problem with and enjoy the quick stress relief that comes with it.

You Should Laugh More

The benefits of laughter in coping with stress and for a healthier life are numerous. It is proven that humor is a powerful tool for stress relief. Try and laugh and be cheerful despite the tough times. Laughter has a way of rubbing off on others so if you are happy, those around you will follow and you will be surrounded by happiness. A happy life is a stress-free life.

Laughter enhances oxygen intake and stimulates the functioning of body organs like the heart, brain and lungs. Your heart rate is also improved for better blood flow and cardiovascular wellbeing. By laughing your way through life, you benefit from muscles relaxation and tension relief. Your immunity will be enhanced through release of stress fighting chemicals in the body. All the pain you are suffering emotionally and even physically is reduced by laughter which triggers the production of the body's natural pain killing hormones.

A happy person is a magnet, attracting people for an improved social life and emotional state. So, when you are downcast just smile through it you will feel better. In any case the difficulties will soon pass and with a positive and happy approach you will survive it. Laughter subdues toxic stress attracting thoughts, helps you forget your worries and enables you to concentrate and work on the tasks at hand. Be happy and grateful for the good things in you have been blessed with. Think about them when you are stressed. Laugh and smile as you recollect and be assured of a stress-free life.

A good sense of humor is not a panacea but is it sure to improve your outlook at life, your health and your social standing. A good laugh will do you a lot of good smiles and laugh more- laughter is indeed the best medicine.

Eat Healthy Foods

Food is the fuel and the source of nourishment for the body, an integral part of our general wellbeing and good health. It is important that we eat the right foods and eat well for us to be stay healthy. A healthy body is able to fend off the side effects of stress with ease.

Food and stress are uniquely interwoven. When faced with adversity some people have a sudden craving for food while others will lose their appetite. It is therefore necessary that we know the right foods to eat especially when we are under some sort of stress. When we encounter stress we crave comfort foods such as fats and sugars. These foods are not healthy and cause harm to us and will cause us more stress. To stay healthy and manage stress we have to avoid:

- Consumption of a lot of fast foods because they are unhealthy and more expensive than cooking for yourself, in the long run.
- Skipping meals because it is a catalyst for stress. If you miss meals you are likely to be fatigued and less nourished thus susceptible to stress.
- Too much caffeinated drinks which interfere with your sleep and deny you adequate rest.
- Eating wrong food types. Eat a balanced diet and resist the temptation of eating too much of foods rich in fats and sugars. These foods only lead to weight gain and cardiovascular problems.

A poor diet will leave you with problems of hormonal imbalance and weigh problems – either loss or too much gain. You will develop a weak immune system and are likely to be susceptible to illnesses. Unhealthy eating will also lead to imbalance of the blood sugar which may lead to diabetes. Stress makes your body burn nutrients you consume much faster than normal that is why you should be on a healthy diet. It is wise that you replenish these nutrients to help cope with stress.

Work-life Balance

All work with no play makes Jack a dull boy! This old saying is very true. You need to have some time away from your job to have fun and engage in things that excite you and pump your blood. Most adults who are stressed can trace the source to their workplace because we spend a lot of time on the job. It is therefore important to balance the time we spend working and time for ourselves for a healthier lifestyle.

Work-life balance is about of dividing your time effectively and adequately between work and your private life. If you let work consume most of your time you and neglect or shortchange your personal needs, you will end up stressed. When your personal life is in order, you are less likely to be stressed since you will worry less. Your mind will not be stretched from being divided between what you need to do at work and the personal matters awaiting your attention.

Spend time with family and friends. It is relaxing and healthy for you. When was the last time you went cycling or shopping with your children? These mundane activities are foundation to a well-balanced healthy life devoid of stress. If your private life brings you happiness you will ably face pressures that come your way. After spending time with your loved ones, you need to set aside personal time for things that are self-gratifying. Go for a massage or run a few laps at the neighborhood field, volunteer your services for a worthy cause etc. Such acts are great for boosting your emotionally wellbeing.

If you embrace a healthy work-life balance you will reap the many benefits. Personal nourishment and care is important for overall health. Balance your private and professional life for a stress-free healthy life where you are happier and revitalized.

Write, Pick Up Your Pen and Paper

Another technique of dealing with stress is writing. It is especially encouraged when one is so stressed or depressed. Putting down your experience, feelings and thoughts in a journal is very therapeutic for recovery and for defeating stress. Writing works by clarifying your mind and thoughts and it is a form of therapy in the sense that it compels you to recall events and thoughts of the day on paper to give you a better avenue to analyze and understand what happened. It is also meditative. It slows down your heart as you focus on your writing to stream out your thoughts to paper.

Writing sharpens and stimulates brain functioning and activity to improve your mental acuity and concentration as well as improving your vocabulary. You are therefore better equipped to handle stressful situations. When you write regularly, the stress triggers in your head are disrupted allowing you to better relax and sleep better. You get up well rested and energized. Writing also fights anger by removing the thoughts from your mind to the writing pad, essentially offering you a platform to vent it out.

When you write down your worries and problems it is easier to solve them. Writing allows you to identify what the problem is, think it through over time and most likely come up with a great unrushed solution and avert the stress that you may have. Having a to do list or schedule helps you focus and get organized; you are able to plan in advance to avoid last minute rushes or procrastinations that will only serve to make your life stressful.

Writing will boost your immune system; by slowing your breathing you are able to breathe in more oxygen to better nourish the brain and blood leading to faster healing and an enhanced ability to fight pathogens. Better breathing also strengthens the lungs, which has a positive effect in fighting respiratory conditions like asthma. To reap the benefits of writing for better health and stress relief, it does not matter what you write, the main thing is to be able to jot down your thoughts and review them. You do not have to be a John Grisham! Write down what is on your mind because the healing power lies in you letting out the negative thoughts that are weighing on your mind.

Chapter 9. Using Anger for Good

In this chapter, we will examine how anger does not always have to be negative. We will look at positive methods to channel our anger, as well as different ways that anger can be used productively.

Anger can indeed be used for good. When handled in a healthy way, it can help define our boundaries and improve our relationships. In addition, some of our most impactful social activists have used anger to fuel their work for change. How can you use anger in a constructive way? Here is one process to move your anger into the constructive stage.

Anger is a natural human emotion

Acknowledge your anger, both to yourself and the other person. Remember that anger is a normal, common human emotion we are all allowed to feel. Your explanation to the other person of how you feel doesn't have to be long. Keep it short and sweet. You can say something like, "I'm starting to realize I'm getting annoyed about what just happened."

Figure out how you want to feel after getting angry. If you're using your anger constructively, you should expect to feel positive after getting angry. You may decide you want to feel better about or have a fuller understanding of the person you are angry with. You may decide you want to resolve the situation feeling that you will have less conflict going forward. Or you may decide you want to resolve the situation in a way that leaves both of you realizing that something positive happened.

Be sure to pay particular attention to the problem, not the person. Whatever was the issue that made you feel angry, that should be your focus, rather than resorting to rage about the person who caused it.

This may be hard to hear, but it's important to realize the source of the anger: it's you, and what you believe. Often your anger relates to a mismatch between expectations and reality. For example, if you're angry that your friend isn't listening to you, it's because you believe your friend isn't providing you with the attention you deserve. This may sound challenging, but the effect will be that you feel more in control of your anger.

You also have to believe that you can solve the situation that is making you angry. You can't change the person you're angry with, but you can improve the situation. If this situation has historically been problematic for you, it can be helpful to make a list of all the strategies you have tried in the past to resolve the issue. Now make a list of strategies you have not yet tried. This can open up your thinking toward a more creative solution.

Next, think about how the other person is feeling and how they see the situation. At times our own anger can blind us to taking the other person's perspective; however, once we can see the other person's point of view, it helps us to temper our anger and use it constructively. Approach the situation in a cooperative way, saying something like, "What can we do to find a good solution for us both?" Sharing the burden of your anger lowers its intensity. Whatever you do, be respectful: no sighing, eye-rolling, or name-calling. That will engender negative feelings and decrease the likelihood they will want to work with you to resolve the issue. Venting and letting off steam is not conflict resolution.

However, if you do find your anger beginning to increase again, it is fine to take a break. Just communicate to the other person that you feel progress is being made, but you want to resume the discussion at a later time or date.

Acknowledging that you have made progress is important. It reassures the other person – and yourself – that you are committed to solving the problem and are not simply giving up. Ask how they feel about the progress you have made so far to resolve the issue, and really listen to the answer. If the other person does not agree that progress has been made, accept that, keeping in mind that they may change their mind down the road.

Anger related to past events

What if the person or situation you are angry about happened in the past? What if you have been hanging on to your anger over this issue for years? Is there any hope that you can let go of this anger and move on?

Of course, there is – and it's worth it. Letting go of anger has very positive effects on both your psychological and physical well-being. Whatever your situation is, when you hold onto a grudge, you see yourself as a victim twice: once at the hands of the person who made you so angry, and again at the mercy of your own unresolved anger.

Here are some steps that Dr. W. Doyle Gentry recommends helping you let go of anger related to the past. First, recall who or what triggered your anger, and when did this occur? Second, accept that you are still angry about this person or situation. You can write or say aloud that you are angry, why, and with whom. Rate the intensity of your anger on a scale of one to ten, with one being very mild irritation and ten being the most intense state of rage. Third, accept that your anger is real, and that you have a right to feel it, just like you're allowed to feel happy or sad. Fourth, accept that you are allowed to express your anger, and that it is certainly possible to express your anger in a constructive, healthy way. Fifth, say out loud or write down three to five ways in which your life will improve once you let go of your anger. For instance, you may feel that the person finally no longer has any control over you. You might stop experiencing physical symptoms, such as stomachaches or headaches. Sixth, make a decision about how you can express this anger without hurting anyone – including yourself. You might decide to write about the person or experience and your anger. You might decide to talk about your anger with a trusted friend. You may even write a letter or tape a voice recording directed to the person you are angry with – one you will never send.

Forgiving anger

What about forgiving someone you are still angry at, who you feel deliberately hurt you deeply? Some people resist forgiveness because they feel it lets the person get away with what they did. You might think, "This person hurt me deeply, and I'm just supposed to say that I forgive them and what they did was, okay?" But forgiveness isn't forgetting what the person did. Forgiveness is for yourself, so that you finally feel that this person and the hurt they caused you does not control you or consume your energy anymore.

Here are some key aspects to remember about forgiveness. Remember, it's voluntary. No one can force you to forgive another person. Also, it's a process. Don't expect for you to feel forgiveness for someone who hurt you deeply in just a few minutes. It will take a while. Also, it's easier to forgive someone when you have a support system. Think of at least one person – a relative or a friend – who you can trust to support and encourage you in your journey of forgiveness. Someone who you know has gone through hard times and adversity but has been able to forgiveness themselves would be ideal. But anyone who can support your choice to forgive is a good support person to have.

For many people, the hardest part of forgiving someone is the fact that you need to be willing to give up some things you are used to. You may have become accustomed to thinking of yourself as a victim, thinking you should have taken revenge, or even that you're entitled to a life completely free of any misfortune or stress (which nobody has, by the way). Once you can give up these beliefs, you will be much more ready to forgive.

Acknowledge that this person did something wrong, perhaps very wrong, and hurt you – maybe even purposefully. Acknowledge also that people aren't perfect. We know this intellectually, but sometimes it can be hard not to expect this. People can be self-involved, make mistakes, and hurt others, whether purposefully or not. It is certainly able to forgive someone when you see that person as someone who is selfish, or difficult, rather than your sworn enemy or the epitome of evil.

As far as the belief that forgiving a person is letting them get away with someone – think about what you are getting away from by forgiving them. Are you getting away from their emotional hold on you? Are you getting away from reliving the event over and over, leaving yourself drained? Are you getting away from tension-related stomachaches and headaches every time the person crosses your mind? Are you getting away from hostility? When you forgive someone, you gain back all the energy you were putting toward staying angry at them. Couldn't you use that energy for something more productive, sometime more pleasurable, something that helps you? As columnist Florence Sherlock once wrote, "Holding on to anger is like grasping a hot coal with the intent of throwing it at someone else — you are the one who gets burned."

It should be noted that you should not even try to forgive someone who is hurting you now, or who continues to harm you on a regular basis. You have to be safe and not being actively hurt right now in order to forgive someone.

Famous people with anger issues

Even famous people have had anger issues. Some have even turned to professional help in order to try to learn how to manage their anger. For example, after the singer Chris Brown assaulted Rihanna, got arrested for several assaults, as well as a hit and run, Brown decided to seek anger management treatment. It ended up becoming court-ordered and mandatory for 90 days after Brown left the treatment in a pique of anger. Another celebrity with anger issues is Naomi Campbell. She has had many fits of anger, and in 2006 was charged with assault for hurling her cell phone at her housekeeper. After that, she was court ordered to take classes on anger management. Sean Penn is another celebrity who is notorious for anger issues. He was ordered to take 36 hours of anger management classes after a conflict with a photographer. Lindsay Lohan's father Michael Lohan was charged with domestic violence in 2011. The judge ordered him to take four months of anger management treatment. After the actor Omar Sharif got into a fight with a parking attendant, breaking his nose, he was arrested and had to take a 15-hour anger management class. Jack White of the White Stripes is another celebrity with anger problems. After a fight with Von Bondies' front man Jason Stollsteimer, White pleaded guilty to assault charges and had to pay fines as well as attend anger management courses. Another singer, country star Billy Currington, yelled at a captain and passengers in a boat, threatening the captain, as they passed by his house. He picked up a charge of elder abuse and making a terrorist threat to cause bodily harm; as a result, he had to pay a fine and take anger management classes. The actor Spencer Pratt got into a tiff with someone else who worked in the TV show "The Hills." He was forced to leave the show for a while and take anger management courses.

It can be helpful to look at the history of anger and how ancient people dealt with anger. Seneca, an ancient Roman philosopher who lived from circa 4 B.C.E. until the year 65 C.E., was a Stoic. Our overarching goal in life, according to the Stoics, was to live in agreement with nature, that virtue is the only true good, and is all that is needed to be happy. They felt that to live a virtuous life, you must not have any passions, because passions are, by nature, disturbing for the soul.

Stoics thought that our minds are entirely rational. Of course, we know now that human beings and human binds are not wholly rational. However, it can be instructive to examine what a stoic like Seneca said about anger. He held that anger is not rational, nor productive. For example, if your favorite necklace is stolen, you think that it is a bad thing that it was stolen, and that you have a right to feel angry and emotional about it. But the stoics would say that virtue (by which they meant things like courage, wisdom, temperance, magnanimity, endurance, and justice) is the only good, and vice (by which they meant things like cowardice, folly, injustice, and wastefulness) is the only bad. Therefore, in this example, it is not bad that you do not have your necklace anymore; it was an indifferent incident. Therefore, no emotional or angry response is needed, nor is it appropriate.

According to Seneca's book On Anger, Seneca states his case that in the end, experiencing anger is mostly voluntary, not involuntary. He structured the experience of anger as having three movements. The first movement is involuntary: in your mind, you immediately think it is bad that your necklace was stolen, and physically you may start to feel your heart race or your stomach churn. Seneca thought that this involuntary experience, this first movement, was not anger. You can only get angry once you give consent to becoming angry. Controlling anger is about pausing after that first movement.

His other advice to deal with anger was to keep learning and educating yourself; resist the temptation to take revenge, because when you take revenge, you admit concede that you have been hurt; love other people, because people have such potential to be good; soothe yourself with the color green as found in nature, or by playing music; fix your posture; and try to keep yourself at a difference from quick-tempered people.

Aelius Galenus (his name is often Anglicized to Galen) was a Greek surgeon and philosopher in the ancient Roman Empire who was one of the best medical researchers of his time. He felt that the soul had three parts: the spirited, the rational, and the appetitive. He did not believe in a separation between the body and the mind, which was unusual at the time. Galen thought that the spirited part of the soul is where our passions, such as anger, are located. Passions were thought to be stronger, and more dangerous, than regular emotion. One of his most famous books was called On the Diagnosis and Cure of the Soul's Passion and was a forerunner to what would become psychotherapy. In the book, he discussed the therapist's purpose of giving counsel to people with psychological issues, so that they would be able to discuss their deepest secrets and passions in order to be cured of them.

The yogis, or leaders in the tradition of yoga, think of emotions, including anger, as forms of energy. They are not wholly a physical experience, and not wholly a mental experience. They fall in the middle of the continuum. Anger decreases naturally. As with other types of energy such as heat, light, sound, etc., if we do not repress anger or deny it, it will dissipate.

It should be noted that anger has long played a pivotal role in social justice movements and activism. Great leaders and activists have often said that their anger is what fueled their entry into social justice. Activists frequently identify with the saying, "If you're not angry, you're not paying attention." When they pay attention to things that are going wrong, they want to change them, and they inspire others to change them. However, they know they have to control their anger and use it judiciously, or it will backfire on them. As Martin Luther King Jr. famously said, "The supreme task is to organize and unite people so that their anger becomes a transforming force."

In addition to Martin Luther King Jr., another leader who transformed anger for good was Mahatma Gandhi. He was able to take his own and others' anger and channel it into social action to transform society. He first became an activist after feeling angry about being kicked out of the first-class part of a train due to prejudice. Instead of getting angry personally at that one person that had him kicked out, Gandhi made the decision then and there to devote himself to change the social conditions in society so that it would not happen to anyone else.

What is RULER?

When we have good emotional intelligence skills, we can channel anger fueled by injustice into constructive and peaceful action to improve the world. The Yale Center for Emotional Intelligence has an approach to emotional and social learning that is known by the acronym of RULER. RULER is a way of looking at anger through five important skills needed for emotional intelligence. The acronym is explained as follows:

Recognizing: Recognizing means identifying the anger that many people feel about situations and incidents they read about or hear about in the news.

Understanding: Understanding is realizing that experiencing and observing social injustice is likely to result in feeling angry.

Labeling: Labeling is about labeling anger and other emotions correctly.

Expressing: Expressing emphasizes expressing your anger in helpful ways, as opposed to hurtful or harmful ways.

Regulating: Regulating is about stabilizing one's emotions in order to channel one's anger into powerful and peaceful actions.

If you're trying to figure out whether your anger is righteous anger that can lead to productive change, ask yourself these questions. One question is, will expressing your anger help? If you're angry about something that you can't do anything about anyway, such as the weather, it's not even worth expressing. However, if you're angry over something you have some control over, expressing it effectively may help.

Another question is, do you feel comfortable telling the other person how you feel? If you can be honest with the other person that you are feeling anger or another emotion intensely, so you may have more trouble than usual communicating, it can help disarm the other person and increase their empathy toward you.

One more question to ask yourself is, have you slowed down enough? Remind yourself to pause, collect your thoughts, or take a few deep breaths before responding. As you try to manage your anger in any particular situation, ask yourself as you go along whether your anger is helping or hurting the situation. Keep checking in with yourself.

Another well-established way to increase your emotional intelligence is to use the DeRose Method. The DeRose Method uses four ways to build emotional intelligence. The first is to study yourself: learn how your behaviors, emotional responses, and weaknesses interact with your anger, anxiety or other emotional reactions. Learn how to observe and notice your behaviors and reactions. Figure out which aspects of your personality need work. Second, breathe correctly and effectively to manage your emotions during times of great stress. Do deep, steady breathing through your nose, keeping your ribcage relaxed. This will tell your brain to relax and calm down. Third, use your negative emotions and energy in order to fuel new adventures and take chances. Fourth, transform negative emptions into positive ones.

It is important to realize that the same source in the body that grows anger also grows passion. Passion and anger are connected. "Aware anger" is a term that some use to describe how they channel their anger into social activism to change and improve the world. People like Martin Luther King Jr and Gandhi channeled the power of anger in order to create transformation. By using anger and passion creatively, they were able to organize and inspire others in order to change the world forever.

Chapter 10. How to Shift Your Perceptions to Lower Your Anger

You have probably heard in the past how your perception can change just about everything. Get twenty people into a room and each person will give you a different story about what went on right in front of them. This can be used to your advantage when you are dealing with anger management. If you're able to change the way you perceive things, you will be able to change a lot of things in your life, including the ways that you choose to express anger.

You must also be able to change your emotional balance. Just by changing your perception, you will be able to do a lot to control your anger and then use it in a healthier manner later on. When you can change your perception, your reactions and your actions will automatically change with it.

It doesn't matter which type of behavior you are working with; they will all have a perspective component. How you see yourself, others, and the world will have a huge effect on your behavior. It will help dictate how you will act on external and internal stimuli. While you can't always control the perception of others, you do have control over your own perception.

You may be wondering how powerful perception can be in determining your emotions. Let's look at it this way: your perception of the world and what is going on in it will definitely have an effect on your attitude. If you find that rage and other intense emotions keep blinding the perspective that you have, it will consume all the actions that you make. These actions are in charge of when you want to get even, when you want to prove that you are better than others, and even when you want to prove others wrong. The result that you get when anger starts to taint your perceptions is not pretty.

In addition, your perception of what is happening in your life will alter your emotional state. When you feel happy, you will often see things in a more positive light, regardless of what is actually going on.

On the other side, when you do not feel happy, your view on things will become even more negative.

While you are not able to affect the perception of others, you can still do something to influence them. As humans, we often worry about how others see us. We don't want to be left out, and so we will make adjustments to make sure that the way we act is looked up to by others. There are times when this kind of attitude is actually a good thing, and there are also times when this can be considered a maladaptive practice. It can add a lot of unnecessary burdens, and it won't likely change how others view you anyway. This adds to more frustration, and you may end up with more anger because of it.

To make things simple, it is crucial that you start to shift your perception so that you can start taking control of your internal emotional state and the issues with anger that come from it. You are not able to change the situations that happen to you, but you have all the power in the world to learn how you should react to them. For example, if someone is making you angry, you don't have the ability to change how they are acting, but you can change how you are reacting to that situation so that it doesn't bother you as much.

You also need to be able to make a conscious effort to avoid the things which are your triggers. Should you find yourself anywhere near them, you need to work on changing how you would respond to them. If you can do both of these, it will be much easier to overcome your issues with anger.

Chapter 11. Anger Counselling

Outrage is a secondary and confounding emotion. As a secondary emotion, anger can have various causes. Passion is established in dread: the dread of the obscure, fear of disappointment and any number of different feelings of dread one may have. Terror is the essential emotion to which outrage is appended. Anger is not an awful emotion; however, it comes to the heart of the matter of outrageous or a wild point; it is presumably time to look for help.

How would you know whether your outrage is wild? If your anger:

- is distancing you from others, particularly your friends and family,
- has demolished or is destroying your connections,
- has to lead or is driving you to physically and emotionally harmed others,
- has to lead or is forcing you to be a social and legitimate inconvenience,
- is the most significant supporter of your grief, or
- Makes you deny you have an issue with it. At that point, your outrage is something other than an emotion, and it is an unmanageable issue. Living in resentment is the poor quality of life and no chance to get in which different people who adore you need to see you live. Luckily, there are approaches to manage outrage issues profitably through advising.
- Outrage advising re-shows the mind to respond reasonably to possibly dangerous circumstances. An annoyance counselor energizes positive self-talk and self-assessment, talking and assessing oneself usually to overcome a situation in which outrage emerges. Different methods presented in annoyance directing may include:
- instructing oneself to require some investment outs to diffuse a displeasure actuating circumstance,
- taking part in physical exercise to discharge endorphins,
- actualizing unwinding systems, for example, profound breathing or yoga,
- utilizing diversion to diffuse hazardous conditions, and

- other ways of dealing with stress chose in the advising procedure.

Outrage does not need to control you or your life. If your annoyance is controlling you or getting to be unmanageable, the time has come to get help. Living in annoyance harms you, yet everyone around you. It doesn't need to hurt. Outrage can be a gainful and helpful emotion when taken care of accurately. Discover how to utilize your annoyance and dread to enable you to carry on with a superior life as opposed to giving it a chance to use you.

Control Your Anger with Anger Counseling

How about we face a few actualities - life will dependably have times of pressure. Due dates at work; budgetary issues at home; coldblooded drivers on the turnpike; inconsiderate laborers at the store - on some random day, numerous sorts of components can combine and make you have an inclination that you need to shout. In any case, indeed a few people can serenely deal with their ordinary disturbances and burdens, while others aren't.

Even though outrage is a consummately normal emotional reaction to certain everyday circumstances, any furious sentiments that are left unchecked can harm connections just as one's close to home wellbeing. Outrage, the board, can be thought of like the way toward controlling your emotional sentiments only as of the physical reactions to those emotions, including raised circulatory strain and an expanded dimension of adrenaline. For specific individuals, managing their annoyance can be similarly as simple as strolling into another space to unwind, or taking a full breath and tallying to ten. For different people, making a fit of anger, the board class might be the best arrangement.

Notwithstanding the sort of individual, you are, the principal determinant to your prosperity is you! If you are not willing to take an interest in a class, at that point the majority of the anger directing on the planet won't help you by any stretch of the imagination. If you need to figure out how to adapt to your resentment flare-ups and restrained irate emotions, at that point just through being completely open with others would you be able to guarantee that you will effectively total treatment?

Finding outrage the executive's treatment isn't troublesome, because there are without a doubt many gathering treatment classes accessible everywhere (even free courses). The free ones won't more often than not be promoted, because of the humiliation it might cause for a portion of the general population who go to these sessions. When you look on the web, there is a decent shot that you can locate a couple of areas where these sorts of classes are being held. Your family specialist may likewise have the capacity to prescribe a spot you can go to.

Outrage Management Counseling

Every individual encounter outrage on different occasions for the duration of their lives, and this is splendidly typical. Anger the executives directing usually is just vital when somebody is crazy and allows their annoyance to control their activities. Outrage is an emotion that can fluctuate in degree; from being irritated to spiraling wild into attacks of fierceness. It isn't the way that we have anger that is the main problem, and it's how we manage outrage in our lives that decides whether outrage is an issue. At the point when scandal begins controlling how individual demonstrations or acts, and after that drives this individual to end up savage or forceful, outrage directing ought to be considered.

At the point when left unchecked and uncontrolled, outrage can prompt serious issues in each part of an individual's life, including connections, and here and there even constitutional issues. Scandal the board guiding can help keep somebody from accomplishing something cruel and reckless that they generally wouldn't have done. It's smarter to get guiding than to plan something unalterable for somebody you cherish and need to live with it for an incredible reminder. A ton of times individuals with indignation issues feels like they are vulnerable and there's nothing they can do to gain power. With annoyance the board advising they can oversee this incredibly ground-breaking emotion known as displeasure.

Much the same as bliss, bitterness, and jealousy, and love, outrage is an emotion that can be communicated in a wide range of ways. Changes in the body happen when somebody encounters and passion. They are both organic and physiological commonly, and effects affect the body.

Generally, they incorporate an expanded pulse that is brought about by an expansion in adrenaline. If somebody is crazy, which means they can't control their reaction to these changes, the normal response of their body dominates. If they have a natural inclination to turned out to be loaded up with wrath and threatening vibe while encountering outrage, their body indeed dominates, and there is nothing they can do about it. A few people even dark out when they become excessively angry and go into wrath or anger, winding up savage and sinister, and they don't recall a thing. Outrage the executives advising is unquestionably essential if this happens.

There are numerous signs that an individual show when they are crazy with regards to outrage. They frequently lash out at the individual or individuals who have made them turned out to be furious. Wild shouting or crying is regularly connected with resentment issues. Knee jolting is an automatic reaction to outrage. Here and there an individual that is chafed with resentment will have flushing skin, just as shaking or trembling. Likewise, when somebody is furious, they can make substantial mischief themselves as well as other people.

If you or anybody you know to experience any of these activities or reactions because of anger, it might be essential to look for annoyance the executives directing. There are no fast goals, yet with assistance and direction, outrage the executives is conceivable and can get you back in charge once more.

Anger Management for Kids for When Things Get Out of Hand

Children are generally not frank concerning sharing sentiments and emotions. A child could be troubled with feelings of agony and blame yet it is improbable that you will take in this from him in a discussion. A tyke will, in general, demonstrate his sentiments by his conduct. When he is tragic, a youngster will presumably remain independent from anyone else and not have a lot to state. At the point when liable, he keeps away from the organization of individuals and would stay in his room. At the point when a youngster needs outrage the board for children, they break their toys, shout as well as pitch fits. Kids are not always vocal in connection to what they are feeling, yet his activities will say what his words are most certainly not.

At the point when kids show outrage, by propelling off into attacks of the fierceness and tossing themselves about on the floor in fits of rage, he needs to experience the way toward realizing what outrage the board for children can instruct him. These activities are signed presents on a parent that this youngster needs assistance. When untreated, this issue could form into a sea brimming with future trouble. Outrage the executives for these youngsters is accessible, and it is successful in dealing with their problems with annoyance. Finding the best displeasure, the executive's assets for children calls for research and experimentation. Different assets give tips about the inconvenience the board to kids. There are motion pictures, books, and a lot of other accommodating data that can be found on sites on the web. If you are worried about a youngster who experiences difficulty concerning outrage, you should look at a portion of the available web assets.

Helping a kid handle his emotions may include unique projects that are focused on children. A tyke won't profit by a grown-up annoyance gathering, and they won't benefit by taking an outrage the board course. These suggestions while brilliant for grown-ups are unreasonably experienced for a kid. Their brains have not sufficiently grown for them to have the capacity to disclose their sentiments to other individuals yet. In all trustworthiness, they may not comprehend what is happening themselves. A counselor does not anticipate that a tyke should open up and educate him concerning his positive emotions which makes him furious. These subtleties are found through a scope of exercises that show outrage the board for children.

Children react well to activity exercises so including amusements in their treatment is probably going to be a savvy begin to outrage the executives for children. It is better than they are encouraged positive qualities and satisfactory conduct through the diversions than it would be for them to complete a one-on-one session with a counselor. When they are given worksheets, shading books, tests, and riddles the displeasure, the executives for children in a split second ends up fascinating and charming. At these occasions, kids could be taking an interest in a program and not understand it. Outrage, the executives, is a troublesome plan to disclose too little youngsters. Considering the way that youngsters are uninformed of their religious sentiments and are not prepared to think rapidly and support their choices, it is tough to encourage them successful exercise plans which require coherent reasoning.

Outrage, the board for children, is fundamental. A tyke needs to figure out how to act legitimately when in various circumstances. The must realize that it is consummately fine to be irate. However, they likewise need to comprehend that this outrage ought not to be utilized bad. Instructing youngsters anger the executive's aptitudes right off the bat in life will give building squares to their future. By rehashing exercises and practices, kids, in the long run, learn outrage the executives for children.

Concerning your children, however, if you need him communicating his resentment appropriately in under 48 hours, go to my site, I have free recordings that are stacked with data to that discloses to you progressively about it.

Anger Management for Kids

Outrage Management for Kids is more earnestly to deal with than at any other time since youngsters like to learn by watching others. What's more, today, as a result of the Internet, TV, PCs and computer games, there are many negative or sketchy icons that youngsters need to adjust with.

It's tough to show kids how to control and deal with their annoyance. First and the most vital assignment ought to look for the wellspring of the fierceness. The most severe issue happens when that equivalent source is something in the house.

Most clinician guarantee that finding the wellspring of annoyance is the ideal approach to begin controlling outrage of a tyke. Well established certainty is that the vast majority of kids don't realize how to control their resentment and express their emotions. Youngsters are entirely flighty, so one ought to get into their heads when attempting to manage their outrage.

To begin with, attempt to find the issue. Outrage the executive's systems for children won't tackle anything if you don't chip away at them. Discover genuine reason for annoyance. Obvious causes are single child rearing, absence of correspondence among guardians and tyke, divorces and so on. Try not to think like a grown-up when you are endeavoring to discover issues. Children see the world in a specific manner.

Furthermore, remember that counteractive action can stop all outrage issues. Talk, talk and chat with your tyke. Speak with your youngster on a similar dimension. Attempt to clarify them genuine issue. Give them a wide range of points of view. Attempt to drive them to consider the matter and their conduct. Topics ought to be explained when tyke understands the wellspring of the issue. With consistent correspondence, you will most likely control your youngster's resentment and fierceness.

Anger Management for Children - 7 Tips That Will Work Today

The central inquiry that numerous guardians have with regards to child rearing is "How would I grow great outrage the executives for youngster's aptitudes?" And although there are a few approaches to taking care of an irate tyke who won't comply with their parent, these seven hints will come path in helping guardians gain the power they are urgently looking for.

1. Never show emotion - Showing emotion will add fuel to a hot flame. Youngsters can detect irate emotions from their folks, and consequently, they will prove considerably more resentment.

2. Realize your outrage triggers- - What is it your inclination directly before you have an angry tirade with your youngster? It's critical to realize your tipping focuses.

3. Acknowledge what's your shortcoming - Parents who acknowledge obligation regarding the battles that happen in their house are bound to defeat the circumstance since they can concoct arrangements on the most proficient method to address it.

4. Relax- - Parents who practice unwinding methods are rationally arranged to manage undesirable fiendish practices that youngsters show.

The way that they aren't effectively enraged will have a quieting impact on the tyke who urgently need positive results.

5. Look for arrangements - Parents who look for answers for displeasure the executives for kids will more often than not discover them. This might be expert advice, or it might be as a child-rearing help gathering.

6. Get familiar with the specialty of exchange - Parents who understand that to get what they need, that they should quit any pretense of something, realizes how to get their children to react decidedly.

7. Overlook offensive conduct - If your child's behavior is a reoccurring issue, it is because they have discovered that their terrible behavior stands out enough to be noticed. When the action isn't hazardous, overlook it. Your tyke will find that the conduct isn't working.

Outrage the executives for youngsters isn't instructed in the present high schools, so tragically guardians understand that they need preparing in this imperative zone when the issue is a 55lb, crying, hollering, gnawing kid who will not return the Hershey's sweet treat. With tolerance and a longing to learn, guardians are furnishing themselves with the information they have to reestablish request.

Chapter 12. The Humble Approach

Did you know that volunteering can really help to mold your character? Whatever it is, whether it's helping homeless people or working at the local dog home, whatever you give in the way of pure volunteerism helps you to feel better about life and better about who you are. Let me show you what it's all about.

My mother gave me a college education because she wanted me to do well in life. That's what most parents want for their children. However, she attached strings. That's not true giving. When you attach strings and expectations, what you do is invite disappointment because your ambitions for your children may not turn out to be their ambitions. One of the reasons I was so angry at life was because I wasn't living the life that I wanted to live. I was always reminded by my mother of my responsibilities toward her. I learned all about volunteerism at a young age and decided that the line of work that I wanted to do was in third world countries where people had lost their homes and had nothing. This wasn't in line with my mother's wishes, but I felt so pulled in that direction that I eventually gave in to my own wishes.

When you volunteer, you give part of yourself to someone else with absolutely NO EXPECTATIONS at all. As I worked with people who I wanted to work with, I found the greatest satisfaction in my life was drawn from giving. It helped me to appreciate life from another viewpoint and it helped to strengthen my character. Why am I here today talking about anger? I suppose that I could say that my anger toward my mother was making my life a total misery. This was anger that was suppressed because I didn't want to hurt her feelings. I just didn't want the life she had lined up for me. I found my joy in giving. When people volunteer, it humbles them and it makes them see life from a totally different perspective. Instead of having expectations of people and being constantly disappointed, you give because you want to give, and your reward is a million times more than the reward you get from giving with strings attached. You feel whole. You feel that your emotions are under better control and when you see the appreciation on the face of someone you helped, you also feel humbled by it. Even if you choose to work with dogs, when you see that face looking up at you and wanting something you have to offer, it's humbling.

I think that you need to experience this to understand it. If you feel that your anger at the world is getting you down, try volunteering, because for once in your life, you are doing something that you want to do and are expecting nothing from it. Instead of getting nothing, you get a feeling of humanity inside you that you can't really experience until you try to give without strings attached.

I learned that you can transfer that feeling into your life. Whereas someone would inevitably make me mad, I would return that gesture with a little kindness that was unexpected. For example, my mom hated the fact that I chose the line of work that I did, but when I visited her, I showered her with the love a child shows, and I gave her flowers. I knew that if I played my life in the opposite way to anger, what would eventually happen is that people around me would accept that this was who I was and that the fact that others have different opinions doesn't really matter that much. As long as I was able to live the life, I felt was doing me the best, then being nice to people who disagreed was simply an extension of that.

Emotions are very hard to cope with sometimes, but when you learn a little about volunteerism, you certainly find your strengths, and your inner strengths are those that stem anger and make you too strong to display it anymore. Do you think people respect you for shouting? They will respect you more and will respect your opinions more if you simply live and let live and accept that the only life you are responsible for is your own. If you have children, you are only a caretaker during their growing years. You can't dictate their futures. Each individual person on the earth is responsible for themselves. If you allow people to make you angry, you show your lack of self-restraint and the only person that hurts at the end of the day is you.

Anger solves nothing. Do something nice for someone you would otherwise not like very much, and you learn to be humble. If your neighbor's dog has been barking all night long, volunteer to take the dog for a walk. You gain a friend and that friendship you make may even influence your neighbor to be a little more caring toward the dog, which may just result in the dog being calmed down at night by a neighbor who begins to care about you. Everything goes around in circles and anger achieves absolutely nothing at all. Try it and you will see that your anger levels are more controllable.

Chapter 13. Simple Anger Management Techniques

Take a minute, a deep breath and slow down

Many times, when people feel angry, they start moving and working at a furious pace. They speak faster, drive faster, move faster, all in response to the fight-or-flight reaction our body feels as a response to increased adrenaline from an emotional or physical trigger.

When you pick up the pace like that, you sometimes forget to slow down and take a look at the big picture. Instead, you jump into that argument with every intention of drawing blood.

The next time you get angry and ready to argue or fight, force yourself to slow down and take a deep breath. Actually, take 3. Breathe deeply, in through the nose, and then exhale slowly through the mouth. The increased oxygen has a calming effect on your nervous system and will counteract that adrenaline that's rushing through your body that makes you want to kill someone. This will also give you time to calm down and assess the situation properly and find a better way of handling it.

Take a step back

When you're involved in an angry situation, your first response is to jump in and attack. But your best choice is to step back and reflect on what's really happening. Rushing in with an angry response will only escalate the conflict and provoke an even angrier response. Let the other person have their say and try to understand their point of view. Seeing the big picture is much easier when you step back from the situation and the anger that may be inhibiting your communication.

Take a break

Sometimes it might take more than just stepping back from a situation. Stress may be igniting several peoples' fuses to the point where everyone is angry and confused. If you're at the point where no one is thinking clearly, it may be best if everyone just goes their separate ways for awhile.

Depending on the size of the problem and the time necessary for all involved to cool off, you could meet back up in 10 minutes or reschedule the discussion until everyone has had time to get their emotions under control.

Watch an instant replay

When you start feeling your anger ready to erupt, take a look back at what led you to this state. Was it something someone said? Or is it something that happened in the past that's triggered by a current issue? Give yourself time to admit you're upset and then to figure out why. Once you know why you're upset, it will be easier to come up with an effective and appropriate solution. You may have to replay the scenario a few times to understand why it's making you so angry. Once you come to the root of this anger, you may even eliminate it entirely.

Put yourself in their shoes

The next time you start to get angry because your child didn't tidy his room, put yourself in his position. Literally. He's much smaller than you and he doesn't have the dexterity yet, to handle making those perfect hospital corners. Did your husband forget to pick up milk on his way home from work? Walk a mile in his shoes and see if you'd remember to stop at the market after the busy day he just had. If nothing else, put yourself in their shoes to see what it would feel like to be on the receiving end of your anger day in and day out.

Take a walk

If necessary, go for a walk for 10 minutes to work off your anger rather than take it out on someone else. Take your dog for a walk, stroll around your block or head out to the park to stretch your legs. Exercise of any kind relieves stress, and your anger will drain along with the stress. Avoid walking like you're on the way to kill someone, though. Walking rapidly may actually feed your anger, especially if you continue brooding while you're walking. I know it sounds cliche to tell you to stop and smell the roses, but you'll find that if you do, or look up at the sky, or notice the birds in the trees, your anger will almost instantly evaporate simply because you've redirected your thoughts.

Once your anger dissipates, you'll be better able to find a solution to whatever the problem is that made you angry, to begin with. Regular exercise is a wonderful way to eliminate stress and if you can get in the habit of walking several times a week, you may notice your bouts with anger getting fewer and fewer.

Talk to Someone

You cannot expect to change without having help from the people you are closest to. If you are working towards changing yourself, create an environment that supports you through every step of the way. Your support could be anyone from your family, friends or a support group. Sometimes along the way, you might lash out at the people who are your support. If you think your support cannot handle it, find an anger management support group where you will not be judged for your anger. The anger management support groups will help you list out the reasons why you are angered easily. They listen to everything you have to say and also encourage you to come out of the problem. They also give you tips for improvement if necessary. When you are picking your support, please keep the following in mind:

1- First and foremost, the person should be someone you would not hesitate to ask for help

2- You have to be able to completely trust the person you will choose

3- You should be able to confide in them without the fear of being judged.

4- You should not fear about asking for help. You are acknowledging the fact that you need help in being able to control the anger. It does not make you inferior to any other person by any means.

Learn to listen

When you feel yourself getting angry with someone, listen to what they have to say. Many people SAY they listen but all they're really doing is keeping their mouth shut while the other person speaks and plotting what they're going to say next when it's their turn again.

Get a pet

If you can't keep a goldfish on your desk at work, then get a puppy, or a kitten, or even a guinea pig for home. Even if you CAN keep a goldfish at work, get a pet for home. A pet gives you a sense of companionship and responsibility.

Interacting with a pet helps relieve stress and calm your nerves. Relieving stress and anxiety helps control anger outbursts and managing your anger becomes more important when you have someone dependent on you to look after.

Wear a happy face

The next time you feel yourself getting angry, just smile. I know, it sounds stupid. But try it now. Smile and hold it for 5 seconds. It's hard to stay upset when you're smiling, even if it's forced. It's even harder for someone to stay upset with YOU if you're smiling. Not only will you calm yourself down, but you'll also diffuse all the other anger, too, with something as cheap and simple as a smile.

Chapter 14. Anger and lifestyle

Studies have revealed that if a person is able to identify and label emotions in a correct way, and also talk about them in a straightforward manner to the point of feeling understood; it is easier for him/her to make negative feelings dissipate. Consequently, the psychological arouse that occur from such feelings also disappear dramatically.

However, when the society is unable to look at anger constructively thus deeming it totally unacceptable, people stay in a state of emotional arousal because they cannot label what they are feeling as anger. We become unable to pay attention to the things going on around us. Further, we are unable to constructively express anger.

The denial makes us unable to understand and regulate our behavior because we stay focused on the inner emotional state. In fact, we tend to experience excessive physical arousal in situations where negative emotions are involved. However, because of the taboos, we do not show any external signs of anger or negative emotional response. Imagine how confusing that is for a friend or spouse. It is also confusing for us.

In some cases, however, we experience feelings of relief after opening up and sharing with someone about our anger and its cause. Psychologists say that this kind of intense relief is experienced because, instead of venting OR expressing ourselves in an unconstructive way, we acknowledge the circumstances leading to our emotional state and constructively work towards finding a solution.

And that positivity points towards the benefits of anger. It acts as a motivator for us to change. Anger encourages us to speak about the things bothering us and find solutions.

However, people with anger management issues (getting angry often) can become ill because of the unregulated physical reactions. Just like stress left unmanaged, anger too can make a person ill. Basically, our bodies do not have the capacity to handle excessive levels of cortisol and adrenaline especially if these hormones and chemicals are constantly released.

Some of the problems that may occur because of regular anger occurring over long periods of time include:

- Sleep problems
- Skin disorders
- Problems with digestion,
- Aches and pains more so in the back and head,
- The reduced threshold of pain,
- High blood pressure which might lead to cardiac arrest and stroke
- Impaired immunity,

Anger may also lead to psychological problems including:

- Depression
- Alcoholism
- Self-injury
- Substance abuse
- Eating disorders
- Reduced self-confidence
-

Some of the key things you should note about anger being unhealthy for you are.

- Chronic anger will increase your chances of getting a stroke or heart attack. It will also weaken your immune system.
- The best ways to deal with anger immediately include taking deep breaths and walking away.
- In the long term, anger can be managed through identifying its triggers, changing your reactions and seeking professional help.
-

Anger can be good when expressed in a healthy way and addressed quickly. In fact, under certain circumstances, anger can help one to think rationally. However, unhealthy anger will wreak havoc within your body and also to the people around you. When you hold anger in for long periods, it will explode into a full rage. If y has unhealthy episodes of anger or are prone to losing your anger every so often, below are some of the reasons you should learn anger management.

- **Anger outbursts put your heart at risk.**

Research have revealed that anger outbursts affect a person's cardiac health. How so? Basically, in the first two hours after an outburst, your chances of getting a heart attack double. This research was found to be truer in men. Anger is physically damaging.

If you fail to express anger in an appropriate manner, it becomes some quiet poison in the body. Gradually, repressed anger will explode and might lead you to an early death. Researchers found that people who are more prone to anger (and that anger becomes part of their personality) are at a higher risk of coronary disease compared to those who are less angry.

To protect your ticker (heart), it is important to identify and address your emotions and more so anger before they go out of control. Basically, everything in excess is poisonous. However, it is important to note that constructive anger is not associated with heart diseases.

Constructive anger involves that which you speak directly to the person that is upsetting you and identifying a solution. It is the kind of anger that makes you more rational.

Anger increases your chances of getting a stroke.

If you have a challenge of controlling anger and you keep lashing out at people for every other thing, beware. One study revealed that people with anger management challenges are at three time's higher risk of getting a stroke. How? You may ask. During the two hours following an anger outburst, there are chances of getting a blood clot in your brain and bleeding within the brain to death. For those with an aneurysm in one or more of the brain arteries, there is a six times higher chance of rupturing it after an outburst.

The good news is that one can learn how to control these explosions. First, identify your triggers, and then learn how to change your responses. Instead of letting your anger control you, do some exercises, change your environment, use assertive communication skills, and learn some other anger management skills to stay in charge.

- Anger weakens your immune system

If you are angry all the time, you might have noticed that you get ill often. The confused state of your body that occurs when you are angry interferes with the levels of the antibody immunoglobulin A. These are the body cells' first line of defense against illnesses and anger issues lower them for at least six hours after an outburst. If you are habitually angry and keep losing control, protect your immune system through several coping strategies including effective problem solving, assertive communication, through restructuring and humor. You need to get away from the black and white mentality and be more open to the opinions of others. Remember that agreeing with the opinion of another person does not make you a loose. Letting another person have his/her way does not make you weak. Either way, you have to start staying calm for the sake of your immunity.

_ Anger problems make a person anxious.

Lack of control makes you worried though you may not notice. Anger and anxiety go hand in hand. One study conducted in 2012 revealed that anger can worsen the symptoms of generalized anxiety disorder. This condition is characterized by uncontrollable and excessive worry that interrupts the normal life of a person. People with GAD were found to have higher levels of anger and also hostility. This anger was mostly internalized and unexpressed thus contributing more to the severity of the anxiety problem.

- Anger has also been linked to depression.

Anger, aggression, and depression are connected. According to numerous studies, these three states are interconnected especially in men. Most people suffering from depression have passive anger – that is, a form of anger whereby a person ruminates about the issue at hand but hardly takes action. The biggest problem with this kind of anger is that it pulls the person deeper into the cycle of depression. Psychologists advise that when one is struggling with depression, he should get busy in order to avoid over-thinking about things.

Any activity that gets your mind off the thing's brewing anger is advised. Get involved in biking, golfing, painting, singing, or any other thing that draws your mind away from anger. These activities tend to fill your mind up and draw it to the present moment. There is no more room for you to brew anger once your mind is occupied by other things.

- **Anger can hurt your lungs.**

If you thought that smoking is the only bad practice that might hurt your lungs, here is some news. Being perpetually angry can hurt your lungs. Anger leads to hostility which in turn affects the capacity of your lungs. Research conducted by Harvard University scientists over eight years about anger and its effects found that people with chronic anger and high hostility rates had a lower lung capacity compared to others. The men with the highest hostility rating had a lower lung capacity. Consequently, they were at risk of developing some respiratory problems. The scientists theorized that an increase in stress hormones associated with feelings of anger creates inflammations in the airways.

- **Anger shortens life.**

As the saying goes, happy people live longer. Stress is directly connected to general health. Stress and anger interfere with your lifespan. Research conducted by the University of Michigan revealed that people who held onto anger for long have a shorter lifespan than those who express their feelings in a constructive way.

If you are a person who is uncomfortable expressing his emotions, practice how to constructively share your feelings. If working on your own does not seem to work, seek help from a therapist. A healthy expression of anger is actually very beneficial. If a person infringes on your rights you have every reason to tell them that they are wrong. Ensure that you tell people exactly how you feel and what you need in a firm yet respectful way.

Chapter 15. Taming Toddler Tantrums - Ideas That Work

More youthful mothers and fathers get unnerved when they hear stories concerning the "horrendous twos." Take mettle. However, you can pull through the little child time frame. It's not clear to comprehend the motivation behind why your baby has Toddler Tantrums anyway at this sort of early age, and a tyke is caught up with considerations of themselves. Everything is identified with the person in question and precisely how they feel. Until at long last they are prepared the best approach to appear, each toy or even smidgen of nourishment they see consequently has a place with them.

Little child Tantrum's temper may have an assortment of outcomes. Your primary initially thought may be that everyone is focused on you and your shouting small child, anyway, getting awkward probably won't quiet the circumstance. Aside from, being a parent, you have a lot more a long time including cramped conditions to foresee civility of the youngsters. So, worrying by what some others think amid this Toddler Tantrums is in reality prone to stress you subsequently aggravating you certainly feel.

Peruse on for specific plans to enable you to adapt amid Toddler Tantrums:

1. **Dismissal the Toddler Tantrums.** This framework is in a perfect world appropriate for when at your home. In public places, you honestly would prefer not to ever leave your youngster unattended as a kind of punishment. Extraordinary conduct in public begins in your own home. Disregarding a little child won't be intense. When your little one is typically squirming on the ground yelling for a bit of nourishment, carry on addressing these as though you never took note. In the end, they will get the indication and quit shouting.

2. **Maintain a strategic distance from quick fulfillment.** In broad daylight, babies pitch fits when they are denied something that they wish. A few guardians offer up to keep their youngster calm anyway a youthful tyke finds quickly. Baby Tantrums will keep on as long as they probably

are aware you may give. Mostly let them know "no" and continue moving.

3. **Try not to get angry.** When you shout thus, they yell your circumstance is fiercely turning wild. You'll finish up crying, and your little child will positively scream. In various occurrence, higher voices mean acculturated visit is done in help of fundamental base senses. Try not to return to the times of early man. Continue utilizing the equivalent peaceful voice you have when they're carrying on for getting your youth to unwind as well.

4. **Compliment your little child after they act appropriately.** Uplifting feedback is desirable over awful. Without great thought, a youthful tyke may work seriously to procure some specific consideration using any means. Carrying on out and throwing tantrums can be a sob for an account. Genuinely don't give it a chance to get to this point. Applaud and commend whenever they will continue to the potty appropriately and when they place away from their toys. Bad habits, for example, expressing "please" just as "thank you" merit a grin alongside a hand applauds also.

5. **Oversee errands following nap time.** Children get punchy if they get depleted. A baby gets into mischief regularly in the fact that they are pulled all-around when they are tired.

6. **Convey treats with you.** Decreased glucose levels can cause Toddler Tantrums. If you are out for a more extended time than foreseen just as lunch or supper time is close nearby, enabling them to eat a sound crunch to keep their craving torments under control and furthermore sugar goes consistent.

7. **Be reliable in your discipline.** At home, you could utilize "opportunity" to manage the Toddler Tantrums for unfortunate propensities. In public places do likewise. Sit your child or little girl on the table for a couple of minutes or take them towards the vehicle. In the long run, they'll discover that you aren't a sucker and they'll begin to behave.

Chapter 16. Anger Management Test

When taking an anger management test, one thing that you should not forget is that anger destroys relationships. With these 25 questions, you will be able to find out if you have anger issues and hence need anger management so that you can protect yourself and the people around you. You could also take the test on behalf of someone else that you think may have anger issues. You can give your response as a Yes, No or Sometimes.

Questions

- When angry, do you find yourself shouting at people?

- When you are angry at your partner or friend, do you often use derogatory signs or aggressive movements using your hands or facial expressions?

- When angry, do you pretend as though you cannot hear the other person speaking to you?

- Do you continue to hold on to your anger and express it beyond a reasonable amount of time?

- Do you find yourself shouting at people whenever you are frustrated by something that does not even relate to them?

- Are you so quick to criticize others when you are angry?

- Do you find yourself making fun of other people?

- Do you feel anger building up from inside before you can explode with rage?

- When angry, do you find yourself using curse words and insulting words?

- Do you use your body or fist to threaten others that you might hit them or hurt them somehow?

- When you are angry, do you cause the other person to cry?

- Are you violent when angry? Do you find yourself hitting, breaking or throwing things around?

- Do you hold grudges when angry? How long before you can let go of that grudge?

- Do you find pride by humiliating others in public?

- When angry, do you derive pleasure from another people's misfortune?

- If you are in a committed relationship or marriage when you are angry at your partner, do you deny them of their conjugal rights?

- Would you say that you are a short-tempered person?

- When having a conversation with your partner, do you often pretend as though you don't understand what they are talking about just for the sake of making them feel stupid in one way or another?

- When upset, do you find yourself grunting and making sounds?

- Do you make comments that are sarcastic just so that you can hurt the other person?

- When angry, do you find yourself comparing your partner or colleague with someone else or something else just so that they can feel humiliated?

- Do you find yourself brining up past failures and disappointments just so that you can mock the other person?

- Do you tell the other person having an argument with you that they are a mental case or crazy?

- Do you think that your partner fears you?

- When you are angry, do you refuse to talk to anyone about what is upsetting you?

How to prepare for anger management

Being able to learn behavioral skills is one step towards proper management of anger. There are so many resources that are available including this book that you can learn so much about how you can effectively manage anger. However, if learning these anger management skills on your own is not enough to help you keep your cool, you may have to seek professional help as we have already discussed.

Getting the right anger management program for your situation can be tasking. However, there are so many ways in which you can get started in your search for the best program that will understand what you are going through and hold your hand through every step of anger management and personal growth. Some of these include;

Asking your doctor or mental health professional for expert referrals to a counselor or program that will help you through anger management.

It is finding trustworthy online sites for resources and books that will help you through anger management.

You are seeking referrals from people who have been through anger management programs before for the best way to approach the whole issue.

Check with your church or organization through employee assistance programs.

What to expect from an anger management education or counseling programmer

Anger management can be handled through support groups with people who are going through the same situation as you or you may choose to have a one-on-one session with a private therapist. The setting and the length of each course including how many sessions there are for anger management usually varies depending on your needs, the program you enrolled in as well as your professional counselor or therapist. For most anger management counseling, the sessions may last weeks or even months depending on your anger intensity among other factors that they discover during their initial assessment and how you progress.

Beginning anger management

When you get started on anger management, one of the most important things at this stage is trying hard to identify some of the anger triggers as well as ways in which you physically and emotionally express feelings of anger. When you can recognize and manage these warning signs, you are just a step away from controlling them.

Factors that you have to pay attention to include;

Stressors: the triggers that bring anger or make them worse. It could be your child, financial stress, a difficult coworker, a cheating spouse among others.

Physical signs: are the indicators that feelings of anger are rising. They can include such things as; lack of sleep, increased heart rate, driving too fast, clenching your fist or jaw among others.

Emotional signs are also the things that indicate that your anger is rising. These include the feelings of wanting to shout or scream at someone or feelings of holding in what you want to say.

In the process of anger management sessions

From a general point of view, one thing that you have to understand is that counseling for anger management often pays attention to developing specific behavioral skills as well as adopting a defined thought process. The main aim of this is to ensure that you can cope with anger. However, one thing that you have to understand is that, if you have other underlying mental issues such as depression, addiction, and anxiety, you have to work through them if anger management techniques are going to be effective at all.

The main reason why you have to go through anger management counseling is to teach you how to:

- ☐ Manage factors that may predispose you to get angry
- ☐ Identify circumstances that are likely to make you angry
- ☐ Learn specific skills
- ☐ Recognize times when you are not logical
- ☐ Keep your cool
- ☐ Express your feelings and needs in an assertive manner
- ☐ Focus on solving the problem
- ☐ Effectively communicating

Chapter 17. Outcomes

Boosting your ability to manage anger effectively and in the right way has lots of benefits. The most important thing here is the fact that it will make you feel that you are more in control of things when life changes turn up the heat. Being able to recognize your anger and knowing how to express anger more assertively ensures that you keep at bay feelings of frustration. You do not hold on to anger to avoid offending people, but you communicate it constructively while providing that nobody gets hurt in the process.

Therefore, anger management ensures that you;

Communicate your needs effectively

Being able to recognize anger triggers and to even go a notch higher to talk about things that infuriate you helps in keeping your cool rather than stirring you up to boiling point. Knowing how and when to express your frustrations helps so much in ensuring that you are not impulsive. It provides that you choose your words and actions wisely so that you are not hurtful. In other words, you end up amicably resolving conflicts to safeguard your relationships.

Maintain healthy habits

Anger sometimes brings stress and this, in turn, increases the risk of developing health-related problems such as sleep apnea, headaches, cardiovascular issues and high blood pressure among others. Make sure that your anger is under control and does not cause health problems in the long term.

Prevent psycho-social problems associated with anger

Some of these issues may range from depression, problems in the workplace, legal issues as well as divorce or having troubled relationships.

Use your anger to get work done

If you express anger in an inappropriate manner, it can make it quite hard to think correctly. Violence in most cases can cloud our judgments and hence decision-making. When you choose anger management, you get the opportunity to deal with frustrations and anger more fruitfully. In other words, instead of picking fights and being destructive, you can divert that energy into getting work done. That is a decisive action!

Chapter 18. Connect your emotions with values

Your behavior and emotions say a lot about your values as a person, even more than what you say. Emotional intelligence is useless without the right set of values, the two go hand in hand. It is, therefore, imperative for you to connect your emotions with the right values so that you can build your EI. It's like building a house. You need to have a strong foundation or otherwise stand the risk of losing the whole house when it is done and ready. Values, in this case, act as the foundation of emotional intelligence.

A person who does something beneficial but ends up hurting others in the long run is generally doing bad and no good. Regardless of how you view things, values are constant everywhere. So, it is easy to distinguish the right value from the wrong one. It is possible to be emotionally intelligent and still act like a jackass. This is because emotional intelligence is a virtue of understanding your emotions and those of others, but without the right values, it is all meaningless to your life. You will be understanding emotions, yes, but still ignoring them and acting out of proportion.

Some of the values that go along with EI include respect and honesty. You need to respect other people's views, opinions and emotions if you want them to reciprocate. Everyone is entitled to their opinions and so, you cannot always force people to view things in the same manner. Also, everyone has their emotions from time to time and you need to understand them when they show them. Honesty comes in where you don't lie to the next person or rather say something just to please them. You need to strike a balance between comforting someone and telling them lies. Often people misuse the idea of comforting to tell outright lies. You need to be honest with others if you want to gain their confidence. You need to appreciate one truth – bad people can also be emotional intelligent. One good example of this statement is conmen. These are people that are perfect at reading other people's emotions and showing theirs too. If there was a test for EI, then they would most likely score straight A's. However, they don't use their abilities in the right manner as all they do is to manipulate the other person into promoting their personal agenda. They value themselves through you and make it a business.

Everyone has an independent choice of values and emotions, but it is important to consider others too. Unfortunately, we sometimes don't even know it when we choose the wrong values and emotions. This is where emotional intelligence comes in to shape our thoughts and decisions. Our emotions are only the mirror that displays our values. So, for you to live a good life, then you must be sure of your values first. Your energy is harnessed from these values and directed to others through your behavior and emotions. The height of emotional intelligence is knowing your true values and not simply saying them through speech.

Conclusion

Thank you for making it through to the end of this book, let's hope it was informative and was able to provide you with all the tools you need to achieve your goals.

The next step is to get started with your own anger management. Anger is something that we all need to deal with on occasion. We may feel angry that someone didn't do something for us, when someone cuts us off in traffic, when we failed to get a promotion at work, or even when the kids are not behaving. Anger is a natural response to things that are going on around us. But there are times when the anger can get out of control, and it seems to be there no matter where you turn.

This guidebook is meant to give you some practical advice to help you deal with the anger that is going on in your life. We took some time to talk about how anger is a natural reaction that is meant to keep you safe, but sometimes it can be blown out of proportion. We also learned how anger is usually invoked by a trigger, and we learned some of the methods that you can use to help keep your anger under control.

BOOK 2

Description

Anger if not controlled can become a problem and will eventually have an impact on your quality of life. It can destroy relationships in both your personal and work life as people estrange themselves from you. If you find you are snappy all the time, use insults as a weapon, need to hit or throw things or feel you are losing control of your temper far too often it is time to seek help. There are many support groups and therapists that can help you regain control and work through your issues. While it can be hard to admit to or talk about it is important to open up to those closest to you. If they are aware of what is going on with you it gives them the tools to help and support, you may even find support groups of their own to better understand anger management issues.

No one really wants to face their problems especially the deep-rooted ones but if we don't, they will just escalate and eventually snowball into an avalanche. Emotions are the hardest things to get and keep under control unlike physical pain there is no spot you can rub or put pressure on to ease them. We need to understand them, work through them and learn how to cope with them. If you feel your anger management techniques or counseling is not working for you, your anger issues may be an underlying symptom of a mental disorder or old physical injury. A medical professional would be able to diagnose any deep-seated issues you may have.

Children who become angry, aggressive or withdrawn may be having difficulties at school, learning, with their friends or may be having a hard time with bullying. If they will not talk to you it is best to have them see a medical professional or a therapist.

This guide will teach you the following.

- Types of anger
- Signs and symptoms of anger struggles
- Anger Checklist

- Reasons for anger
- How to manage anger using various ways such as; anger counselling, embracing positive self-talks and using anger management tips
- Tips to manage anger-for parents and self-help tips for anger management **AND MORE!!**

Anger should not be confused with aggression, as many may assume. Anger is a mental state as aggression is a behavior made by a person. You might be angry from time to time, but this does not mean you will show aggression. Aggression, in most cases, happens due to the constant feeling of threat and fear.

Introduction

To deal with the hole in the bucket, we must first expound on its meaning. Anger is defined as an irrational emotion that everyone faces from time to time. Experts argue that it is a natural way that the body uses to protect itself from what it considers wrong.

It is provoked by feelings of criticism, frustration, and threat, and depending on the circumstance, it can either be good or bad. The cause of anger is extensive as it can go further to personal differences such as in religion, opinions, and beliefs. It can make communication standstill and so should be avoided if possible. When you are angry, you're more likely to say and do things that you didn't intend. Again, anger is contagious in the sense that it can spread to the next person. For instance, when you are angry at an individual, you are more likely to make them angry too.

Aside from being a primary emotion, it can equally turn out as a secondary feeling that is caused by other mental states such as sadness, loneliness, threat, and fright. Research shows that one out of three individuals has a close friend or relative who has anger issues. This is a study that was conducted by the mental health foundation in the United Kingdom. It also suggests that many people in working environs tend to experience anger due to the compiling of different emotions.

Psychologist T.W Smith argues that anger is an unpleasant emotion that isn't constant in terms of intensity. In this sense, what makes people angry varies from one individual to the other. What may cause ire to you might not bother the next person one inch.

It is often a queer behavior for some people who don't show any feelings or outbursts when angry. As much as this is a good show in public or in front of others, it is harmful to the individuals. Suppressing anger does more harm than good to the person doing so. However, this is not to imply that letting it out without control is ideal. You should know how to manage it and regulate your feelings.

Scientifically, the brain has a small region where anger develops and starts, and it is called the amygdala. It is a part of the brain that processes information that is linked to one's emotions. After doing so, it contributes to some reactions that come in the body. This is through the signaling of chemical production to send commands to the body to be alert. When you are angry, the brain leads to the release of catecholamines, which are neurotransmitters. The two biomolecules that together form catecholamines, epinephrine, and norepinephrine, contribute to making a person angry. When these molecules are released, they give strength and energy to the body in times of threat or fear. This is what creates the adrenaline rush, which is a common occurrence that forces a rapid reaction against something or someone that leads you to anger. It's that superhero feeling you get that sometimes makes you have the urge to fight and at times even prevents you from feeling pain.

The effects of this adrenaline rush include faster breathing, an increased heart rate, and boosted blood pressure. Sweating also arises, and in some cases, the pupil dilates. The increase in blood pressure is meant to get you ready for the confrontation. This explains why angry people mostly have their faces red. Don't mix this up with the typical phrase blood boiling as it doesn't have a literal meaning. There's nothing like the blood boiling up, and if this were to be the case, you would die right away.

Anger relates to thinking in the sense that we can control what makes us angry. In this case, you can withhold your feelings and prevent aggravation if you wish to do so. Scientists argue that the difference between anger and fear is that for anger, the body temperature increases while for the latter, it decreases.

- When one tries to hide other emotions.
- When one sees some things to pose a threat.

When one's expectations are not met or when you feel shortchanged.

A therapist by the name Dr. Potter-Efron Ronald argues that several factors lead to anger. He authored the book "Healing the angry brain," where he shares his thoughts on anger. In his words, he claims that some of the things that lead to anger include drug abuse, stress, cultural effects, frustration, and bodily dysfunctions that are as a result of diseases.

German scientists have also argued that anger can be genetic for some people. Minor mutations knowns as DARPP-32 affects catecholamine compounds that are located in the brain. Martin Reuter, who is one of the research scientists, explains that those without the mutation and others who have "TC" and/or "TT" can't control their emotions. Therefore, sometimes, it is not a person's wish to be angry, but it is a result of the genes.

The heart and anger have a close relationship, and that's why you will notice rapid heartbeats when you are angered. This arises from the constriction of the blood vessels that cause the heart to pump more vigorously. As a result, individuals with the tendency to get angry more often end up getting health disorders and conditions such as heart rhythm disorders and an increase in blood pressure.

The other reason why enraged people usually get unhealthy is due to the increased levels of fatty acids and glucose in the body. Fatty acids, to be precise, lead to the growth of plaques inside the arteries. This results in the thickening of the arterial walls and the narrowing of vessels which can cause a complete blockage. Thus, scientists add that this can accelerate atherosclerosis, which may contribute to strokes and heart attacks. This is why angry people are more prone to heart failure and breakdown, now you know.

Having read all that above, it may occur to you by now that it is relevant to tone down on your anger. It is not that easy to do this, but there are ways you can utilize (presented later in the text) that will help you get it done. This will help you to live an anger-free life that ensures you live a healthy and longer life.

Chapter 1. Types of Anger

There are various types of anger disorders that most people who have difficulty controlling their anger suffer. So many experts in psychology have published a wide range of anger disorders that mostly conflict with each other. However, here, I will discuss only the widely accepted forms of anger for the sake of avoiding contradiction.

Passive anger

These kinds of people often do not even realize that they are angry. When you have passive anger, the emotions that you show often come off as sarcasm, being mean or even apathy. In most cases, such people have been found to engage in certain behaviors such as skipping work, school or even alienating themselves from others. They also perform poorly especially in both social and professional events. People may see you as though you are trying to sabotage yourself even though you may not realize it and may not also be in a position to explain your actions.

Anger can be suppressed at times; it may make it very hard to recognize. In such a situation, the only thing that can be promising is identifying the emotion that underlies your actions so that you can successfully bring the object that is stirring up your anger to light and hence allowing you to deal with it.

Aggressive anger

People who experience this kind of anger are usually aware of their emotional feelings although they may not always understand the root cause of their violence. In other instances, you will find them redirecting their violent outbursts to scapegoats. This makes it quite hard to deal with the real issue. One thing that you have to bear in mind with is that aggressive anger manifests itself in the form of volatile or retaliatory anger. It can lead to physical damage of other people or their property. Therefore, it is very critical to learn how to recognize anger triggers so that you can be able to effectively manage symptoms when they occur and deal with them more positively and constructively.

Assertive anger

This type of anger is one of the most useful examples of a kind in which people use their violence to fuel a positive change. However, this means that, instead of avoiding confrontations or keeping the anger inside, you choose to express it in a way that creates change around you without necessarily being destructive or distressed.

Assertive anger is mostly considered a powerful motivator that helps people achieve their desired dreams in life.

Behavioral anger

With this kind, violence is often expressed physically. Often people with this kind of rage feel overwhelmed by their emotional feelings that they tend to show it by lashing out at objects in anger. It usually is very unpredictable and harms the direction that their lives take after that, mainly because of legal and interpersonal consequences.

With this kind of anger, it is essential that you take a moment to calm yourself down before you do something that you might regret for the rest of your life. You can do this by making yourself away from the situation and using self-talk to ensure that you regain your control.

Chronic anger

This is often a more generalized resentment that is ongoing about other people and directing that anger towards yourself. A habit of getting irritated often accompanies it, and this is often prolonged and can eventually result in adverse effects on your wellbeing.

The best way to control this kind of anger is taking some time to reflect on what may be triggering your anger. Once you have identified the trigger, you are in a better position to deal with your inner conflict by merely allowing yourself to go through a phase of forgiveness for all past transgressions. This process of forgiveness is very critical in helping you deal with hurt and frustrations that you may have been holding on.

Judgmental anger

This is a wave of righteous anger that often is directed to a perceived injustice. Even though this type of rage assumes a moral superiority stance of bitterness that is justified, it may cause you to alienate friends by merely making their opinions invalid.

The best way to handle this kind of anger is by dedicating to explore different situations as this may seem simple only on the surface with underlying complexities. In other words, the perspective that others have can play a critical role in offering you valuable insight into possible solutions to the problem at hand.

Self-abusive anger

This also referred to as shame-based anger. This means that, if you have been feeling a lot more hopeless and humiliated, you may internalize those feelings and express that anger burning from the inside through negative self-talk and harming yourself. Others may resort to disordered eating and substance abuse and end up having low self-esteem and hence alienation from the rest of the crowd.

To deal with this anger, it is important that you employ the help of cognitive reframing techniques to challenge and defeat self-defeating thoughts that you are experiencing. You could also find mindful meditation very useful in dealing with impulses.

Verbal anger

This is a type of rage that is seen as a psychological abuse that aims at hurting those who are believed to cause violence in the first place. It may be expressed in the form of threats, ridicule, criticism, blame, and shouts among other verbal cues. Feelings of shame also accompany this and regret afterward.

Whenever dealing with this anger, it is essential that you think twice about what is going to come through your lips before you utter anything at all. Yes, it may be tempting to blurt out something, but realize that the key to managing that anger is delaying that impulse to lash out in the wake of the moment. With practice, you will understand that you can curb the tendency of verbal abuse and effectively replace that with an assertive expression instead.

Volatile anger

This is the kind of rage that seems to emanate from nowhere specific. Often, people get upset over anything small or big alike. Once this type of anger is impulsive, it also is calmed down almost instantly.

Unfortunately, this kind of anger can be very destructive. This is because people around you will see the need to stay away from you for fear of triggering rage. If not addressed, it may result in destructive outbursts.

To deal with this anger, it is important that you carefully find out what the signs and symptoms are that precede these outbursts. Then see how you can effectively use relaxation techniques to control that anger from escalating and tipping over to boiling points and ultimately exploding.

Anger as a substitute emotion

Did you know that sometimes anger can be a substitute emotion? You may be thinking 'but what do you mean by a substitute emotion?' Well, sometimes, people often drive themselves into anger so that they do not have to deal with their pain. This means that, instead of allowing yourself to grieve your pain away, you replace that pain with anger because it feels better to be angry rather than feeling pain. It may happen either consciously or unconsciously.

Well, being angry instead of feeling pain is something that has lots of advantages, and the main one is a distraction. When you are in pain, all you can think about is your pain. However, if you are angry, it is easy to think about harming those that have caused you pain. In other words, there is an attention shift from focusing on yourself to concentrate on others.

Thus, it is important to note that anger only protects people temporarily from recognizing, dealing with and coping with their real painful feelings. You merely get to worry about revenge. However, the most important thing to keep in mind is that making yourself angry plays a critical role in helping you hide the reality that the situation right in front of you is frightening and is making you feel vulnerable.

Additionally, in as much as anger provides an adequate smoke screen for vulnerability, it also creates certain feelings of moral superiority, righteousness, and power, something that is absent when someone is in pain. In short, when you are angry, you have cause to be angry. In other words, what is going through your mind when angry is that the people who have caused you pain need to be punished. In other words, it is hard to find someone being mad at another person who has not created them harm in some significant way.

So, what are the benefits and costs of anger?

Well, when it comes to anger, in as much as it is a negative feeling, it is accompanied with some benefits such as social, health and emotional. Whether your anger is justified or not, it is that seductive feeling of righteousness that provides a more powerful boost to our self-esteem and soothes our ego.

The truth is, it is often very satisfying to feel angry rather than acknowledge the painful feeling of being vulnerable. In other words, you can only use your anger to turn vulnerability and feelings of helplessness into power and control. For some, developing an unconscious habit of transforming vulnerable feelings into anger helps them avoid dealing with real issues.

However, the problem with this is the fact that even though anger distracts you from the truth (vulnerability), you still are and feel that vulnerable to some extent. In other words, by turning your pain into anger does not mean that your pain will suddenly go away. It only distracts you from it just but for a moment. Therefore, bear in mind that anger does not address the real issue that brought you fear and vulnerability in the very first place, it only creates a new problem that can affect your social, emotional and physical well-being.

Chapter 2. Signs You Are Struggling with Anger

Daily annoyances are driving you crazy

Do you get mad occasionally? Then it's totally fine, but if you find yourself losing it over every little thing that doesn't happen to your liking on a daily basis, you have got a big problem. For instance, when I was dealing with my own anger problems, if my roomie forgot to unload the dishwasher, I would yell at him or give him the silent treatment. If you have a habit of yelling over the phone or find yourself road raging when you fight with someone, it's a strong signal that your anger has become out of control.

Things can get pretty intense with you

You don't just get mad you get really MAD. Now this is what I mean by intense anger. This is also a great barometer for analyzing an anger problem. Be honest with yourself and answer this. How intense do you get when you are angry on a scale of one to ten, ten being extremely calm, with zero being intensely enraged. If you rate yourself anywhere beyond 5, it's time for some heavy damage control.

You tend to hold grudges

Do you still get angry at the slightest mention of an old friend who did you wrong? If a considerable amount of time has passed since the incident happened, and you still can't seem to let go it, you should know that it's extremely unhealthy. Emotions aren't supposed to last more than a few minutes, hours or days. If we are holding on to our angry emotions for much longer than this, it's often called a grudge – something that can eat your peace away.

You get abusive quickly

If you swear at the drop of a hat, or get violent even at the slightest of provocation, chances are that you are a short fuse who can't control his or her anger. If you get to the point of being physically or verbally abusive more than once in a year, it says a lot about your mental state - which is extremely problematic right now. Being out of control is not a feeling anyone enjoys, and you should look at your behavior as an opportunity to change yourself.

You push friends away

If you are always angry, chances are that your friends might hesitate to call you. But it's also possible that you are the one who ends up pushing your friends away because you are not sure how to deal with your frustration. Experts believe that it's quite common for people to isolate themselves while they are trying to manage their anger issues.

Your heart starts racing when you get upset

Do you feel sick to the stomach and feel like your heart is racing? Then there are other physical symptoms such as shortness of breath, profuse sweating or headaches. If you experience these symptoms on a regular basis, it's time to take a serious look at whether it's a medical condition you have, or it is your unhealed anger that's sending such destructive signals.

You feel overwhelmed

Trapped anger can leave you feeling empty. So don't be surprised if you feel exhausted, or unhappy because it's your anger that is causing you to feel overwhelmed. Have you been depressed lately? Chances are that your depression is masking itself and comes out as anger. If that's the case, seek immediate medical help without wasting any more time.

You apologize a lot

While apologizing all the time can also be a sign that you haven't forgiven yourself for something you did, most often it stems from unhealed anger. If your loved ones have been pulling away from you lately, or you spend most of your time trying to make up to them, you anger issues could be getting worst. You may also feel like you spend a large amount of your time fixing your relationships rather than maintaining them.

You are always defensive

How do you react to honest conversations? Are you always on the defensive? It has been observed that people who struggle with anger issues can have a really hard time seeing the big picture, and that causes them to turn defensive even at the slightest of jabs taken at them. And God forbid if someone calls them out for your anger that could mean unleashing all their frustration upon the other person in the worst possible way. Defensiveness is a common way of hiding one's anger or painful emotions from the past.

Your memory is always fuzzy

Anger can affect a large part of how your brain functions. Watch out for cognitive issues. Intense anger can spike your cortisol levels that can quickly turn into memory issues and being unable to create new memories. If you have noticed that you might be suffering from memory issues of late, it's more than time to work on releasing your anger or see a therapist who can help you overcome it. I promise you that you will have a much better life once you get past your anger issues.

When To Ask For Help

For some, anger management is just something one can get over with after a few years. Some would say it just needs maturity or to be exposed more in social activities to develop their way of communication without getting angry or easily offended.

But in reality, there is much more than that. This is not just about getting along with people, but what happens is an internal disturbance that makes us feel irritated and unable to control all our emotions. If untreated, this may lead to a much bigger problem and you do not want to end up in the point of no return, right? Thus, it is very important for one to know when to get help when anger is getting harder and harder to control.

Unable to Control Your Frustrations and Anger

It is normal to be angry. But to lose your ability to control the frustration and anger is a different matter. Keep in mind that there is a very thin line between being angry and infuriated. It is very important that you are self-aware when you are angry so that you can still be able to keep your cool. But if not, then that is already an obvious signal that you definitely need some help.

Experiencing Troubles in Work

We all have our fair share of committing troubles at work. And having an argument against another employee from time to time is just an ordinary routine. But when you get to the point that you have had an argument with all your co-workers including your boss, then you should know better that you are the problem and not them. When you get fired multiple times because of misconduct brought by inability to control your anger, you should already consider looking at your anger management capacities.

Unintended Physical Violence

Violence is not just about hatred or frustration, but it is also caused by anger. If not handled properly, anger can be a destructive force that can hurt or in worst case scenario, kill a person. Even if one does not intent to, when blinded by anger, you may be capable of doing something that you think is not possible. Before doing something, you would soon regret, it is necessary that you ask for help as soon as possible. Sometimes, when anger reaches this stage, it is already a challenge to stay calm and keep your cool. Thus, more often than not, rehabilitation for some time is the best option on these types of condition.

Chapter 3. Checklist For Anger Detection

Common Behavior Exhibited When Angry

All those people who have an angry spirit tend to display the following characteristics:

Using justification

One of the main factors that contribute to the spirit of anger is the misconceived notion that a little anger is perfectly acceptable. Yes, it is true that anger is a normal emotion, but this doesn't mean that you're supposed to hold onto it, nor does it mean you're supposed to let it get out of your control. By allowing a little anger to harbor within you is equivalent to lighting a small flame in a dry forest. Anger certainly tends to alert the fact that something is amiss and that one must proceed cautiously to avoid any situations that can lead to words of potential bitterness. Also, anger might reveal that there are certain unaddressed hurt or grievances in your past which need to be addressed immediately so that you can resolve your feelings of anger. So, allowing even the tiniest bit of anger to linger within you is an unconditional invitation to potential trouble. Therefore, it is never a good idea to justify harboring even a little anger within yourself.

Anger can be controlled

The way people seem to think that a little anger is perfectly fine also to seem to believe that they can control their anger. Yes, you can learn to control your anger. However, when you cannot control your anger, it often transforms itself into ugly emotions like malice, bitterness, or even wrath. Usually, when people talk about controlling their anger, they often refer to their ability to be able to contain the damage that their anger has caused. However, you must understand that one angry response produces a different kind of hurt. An angry person might believe that he can control his anger, and when it turns out that he cannot, it only leads to more anger.

Insensitive to the hurt they cause

A lot of people fail to realize the damage their anger inflicts on others. Once they have had an angry outburst, they simply forget about it and move on. Such people don't stop and think about the damage they inflicted on others. Also, they don't bother to ask others for their forgiveness or apologize for their behavior. In fact, they often feel that their anger was justified and not unwarranted. At times, this insensitivity is caused because of a simple fact that we cannot see our expressions or hear our voice when angry. If you could witness yourself having an angry outburst, you will become mindful of your behavior and response.

Quite indulgent

Those who use their anger as a weapon tend to do so to get their way. A person who is quick to anger will also be quite indulgent. They often tend to do things they like with little or no consideration for others.

Quick to get offended

Those with an angry spirit are certainly quick to get offended. They seem to have a short fuse which can go off at any second. Everything and everyone seem to be able to trigger their anger. Not only do they get offended easily, but they quickly jump into arguments too. A small discussion can spiral into a full-blown argument within no time. They don't have the patience to think carefully and often allow their emotions to guide their behavior.

Cannot forget or forgive

All those with anger issues are incapable of forgiving others or even receiving forgiveness. Not just this, but they also struggle with letting go of things. They hold on to many unpleasant memories, and this can fuel their perpetual anger. Their inability to let go only makes them angrier. If you come across someone who holds grudges about the pettiest of issues, then it is quite likely that that said individual has anger issues. Apart from this, they are incapable of asking for forgiveness. From their perspective, they can never be wrong. This kind of thinking makes them believe that they don't need any forgiveness. A person who cannot control his or her anger will also try to shift all the blame for their anger onto others conveniently. They will go to great lengths to get rid of any responsibility for their behavior.

Harsh on the outside

A person who is susceptible to angry outbursts might seem quite harsh on the outside. However, their anger is usually a means to hide their underlying insecurities. Usually, they tend to use their anger to mask any unpleasant emotions like hurt, guilt, or even sadness. If something makes them uncomfortable, they might seem quite harsh. However, they are quite sensitive and even more sensitive to criticism, and the smallest of issues can upset them.

Anger Checklist

Now that you are aware of the different behaviors exhibited by those who have a problem controlling their anger, it is time to make an anger checklist. Those who struggle to control their anger tend to get angry with others, even strangers and tend to lash out or yell at them to express their anger. This kind of behavior usually interferes with their quality of life and prevents them from leading a happy and calm life. Here is a checklist you can use to decide whether you have any trouble controlling your anger or not.

Do you tend to frequently yell at others when they do or say things that irritate or offend you?

- YES
- NO

Does it feel like others do or say things to irritate you intentionally?

- YES
- NO

Do you easily lose your cool and get mad at others for "breaking the rules?" For instance, when someone doesn't follow the rules while driving?

- YES
- NO

When you get angry, does it escalate quickly?

- YES
- NO

Do you tend to hold onto your anger even after the event that caused your anger is long past?

- YES
- NO

When you get angry, do you lash out at others or even destroy their property?

- YES
- NO

Do you think about ways in which you can obtain revenge against those who angered you?

- YES
- NO

When you get angry, do you experience any physical symptoms like the quickening of your heart rate, warmth in your face, or any tension in your muscles?

- YES
- NO

Do you ever feel like maybe your anger was uncalled for or irrational?

- YES
- NO

Identify the Causes for Your Anger

You can probably think of different reasons that make you angry. You might be angry because a referee didn't call out a foul made by the opposing team. A friend might have stood you up. Your child might not have cleaned his or her room as they promised. Maybe a driver cut you off during the rush hour. You might also be mad about any promises made by the politicians, which they didn't follow through, the prices of gas, and so on. The list of people or situations that can make you angry can go on for a while. However, the two reasons that all these issues can be summed up to are the violation of any expectations you had, or they somehow prevent you from attaining your goals. We all expect fair treatment and get angry whenever we're yelled at for no apparent reason. If you were craving for a soda and the vending machine doesn't work, that can trigger anger. If others don't follow your idea of social norms, it might make you angry. Here is a silly reason that can trigger your anger; perhaps you don't like the idea of people wearing sandals and socks together. If you see this abhorrent trend, it violates your idea of personal taste and can annoy you.

Everyone has different anger triggers, and they tend to vary according to one's age, culture, and even gender. However, an event or a person by itself isn't sufficient to trigger one's anger. There lies a mental aspect wherein we get to decide whether our anger is justifiable or not and who is responsible for it. In the blink of an eye, our mind analyzes who is to be blamed, and before you know it, you are angry. For instance, you might get angry that a driver cut you off during rush hour. Your anger might be justifiable here because the driver was breaking traffic rules. However, would you still be angry if you knew that the driver had a medical emergency to attend to? Well, the way our brains process the trigger result in whether you get angry or not.

If you want to learn to manage your anger, then you must become aware of your anger triggers. It can be an event, a situation, or even a person who can trigger your anger. Once you know your triggers, you can start anticipating your likely response and therefore, you can be a better position to express your anger constructively. In this section, you will learn about the common anger triggers.

Unfair treatment

People tend to feel rather irritated, annoyed, or even slightly enraged when they are treated unfairly or when something unfair happens. Who wouldn't get mad when they are doled out unfair treatment? However, as you know, life is never fair. Unfair events are bound to happen at some point or another. Here are a couple of common instances of unfair events. For instance, someone might cut in front of you in a queue. Your boss might criticize you for a mistake made by your colleague. Your peers might give you a poor work evaluation. You might get a ticket for speeding or jumping the signal even when you didn't. Regardless of whether what has happened to you is truly unfair or not, the one thing that matters is your reaction to it. Is your reaction apt to the situation, was it mild, or completely out of proportion?

Response to pressure

The world that we live in these days is full of different stressors. People tend to feel like they are being pressurized to keep multitasking and constantly increase their productivity. However, there are certain things that are inevitable, will get in your way, and slow you down. For instance, you might get stuck in a traffic snarl after a long day at work, might be running late for an important meeting, might be running late to catch a plane, or have to constantly respond to your family member's texts while busy with work. All these things can make anyone feel quite stressed and frustrated. However, these things are, at times, unavoidable. You can probably set a couple of limits for certain types of specific interruptions. For instance, you can probably tell your family members not to text you while you're at work unless it is an emergency. However, there are different frustrations and delays, which are unavoidable or inevitable in daily life. If you let your anger get the best of you in such circumstances, all it will lead to is an increase your stress and nothing else.

Dishonesty and disappointment can trigger anger

It's quite common to feel upset, annoyed, or angry when someone let you down, doesn't keep up the promises, or exhibit any dishonesty of any kind. Everyone tends to encounter these instances at one point of time or the other, and it is quite normal. For instance, your partner might cheat on you, your best friend might forget your birthday, your children might not like you, your boss might not give you the promotion he promised, a friend fails to keep up her promise to help with your shift. It is quite normal that any of these instances might trigger your anger. It is normal to feel annoyed. However, you must try to analyze which of these events tends to happen to you frequently and trigger irrational anger.

Any threat to your self-esteem

Everyone likes to feel good about themselves. Even a person who has low self-esteem doesn't like being put down and doesn't like being subject to any criticism. At times people might react to any threat to their self-esteem by expressing sadness or even engaging in self-loathing; however, at times, others can respond with anger. Any threat to one's self-esteem can either be real or an imagined one. For instance, receiving a bad appraisal, getting criticized or disrespected, making a fool of oneself in front of others, being stood by a date, or doing something equally embarrassing can be a threat to one's self-esteem.

Experiencing discrimination or any prejudice

History is proof that anger and rage can be transformed into something that can be life changing and remarkable. For instance, Mahatma Gandhi and Nelson Mandela channeled their anger regarding prejudice and discrimination and turned it into a movement to change the world. Whenever a person is subjected to any prejudice or discrimination, they tend to respond with anger, rage, or irritation. The nature of discrimination or prejudice that they are subjected to can be implied or even blatant. Common examples of prejudice and discrimination exist in the form of sexism, racial discrimination, discrimination on the grounds of sexual orientation or any disability, discrimination based on religious beliefs, and so on. Well, this list of common prejudices can go on for a while. It is quite common for anger to be triggered when one is subjected to any intolerant or prejudiced behavior.

Being attacked

Violence has certainly become quite common in today's world. Being the victim of any abuse or violence tends to create anger, and this is quite natural. Some might respond with anger, while others might experience anxiety or even depression. At times, chronic abuse also changes its victims into abusers. Abuse can exist in several forms from being blatantly obvious to subtle. A couple of examples of a broad category of abuse include assault and battery, sexual abuse, domestic violence, verbal abuse, child abuse, any war trauma, or even verbal intimidation. As with discrimination and prejudice, you might either be the victim or the perpetrator. Regardless of the role you play, it does involve a lot of anger.

Chapter 4. Reasons for Anger Management

Costs of Anger

At times, anger is beneficial, provided you address it quickly and healthily. However, any anger when not expressed properly or when it is suppressed for long periods can harm your body. Here are the different ways in which an unhealthy episode of anger can harm you.

Your Heart's health

Anger can have a significant effect on your heart's health. A lot of people are unaware of the physical damage that anger can have on their cardiac health. According to Dr. Chris Aiken of the Wake Forest University School of Medicine, the risk of a heart attack doubles within two hours after having an angry outburst. When you express anger indirectly or take steps to repress it can also harm your heart. A study suggests that those who are prone to angry outbursts or have anger management issues have a greater risk of cardiac diseases when compared to those who don't have any severe anger issues. If you want to protect your heart and improve its health, then you must start addressing your emotions before you lose all control.

Increases the risk of strokes

If you have any anger issues, then you should be aware of this. The risk of an individual having a stroke due to any internal bleeding in the brain or from a blood clot increases three times during the two hours after an angry outburst. It is also said that the risk of rupturing an existing brain aneurysm increases by six times after an angry outburst. However, the good news is you can control these angry outbursts by coming up with positive means to express your anger. By conditioning yourself to express anger in a constructive way can help control your temper.

Harms your immunity

If you notice that you are constantly angry, then your chances of falling sick tend to increase. In a study conducted by scientists at the Harvard University, it was noticed that even the mere recollection of an anger episode from the past reduced the levels of immunoglobulin A for almost six hours. The immunoglobulin A is an antibody, and it usually is the body's first line of defense against any foreign bodies or infections. By developing effective communication skills, using humor, and restructuring any negative thoughts can help regain control of your anger.

Worsens anxiety

Anger tends to worsen anxiety. So, if you are a chronic worrier, then your anger will only worsen your anxiety. GAD or generalized anxiety disorder is a condition wherein an individual tends to experience high and uncontrollable levels of anxiety in their daily lives. Existing research shows that the symptoms of GAD can be exponentially worsened if the individual has any anger issues.

Depression

Anger is a common emotion, but the inability to control it can harm one's mental well-being. It is believed that angry outbursts coupled with susceptibility to anger can cause depression. Also, anger can prevent an individual from experiencing any pleasant emotions. So, it is a good idea to get involved in activities that you enjoy so that you don't have the time to think about your anger, which in turn can change your overall mood.

Hurt your lungs

You don't necessarily have to be a smoker to harm your lungs. Being perpetually angry can harm your lungs according to a study. In this study, scientists at the Harvard University used a hostility scale to monitor the health of 670 men over a period of eight years. The results of this study showed a decreased lung capacity in all those participants who were hostile most of the time. This led the researchers to conclude that the increase in stress hormones due to anger tend to cause inflammation of the airways in your body. A combination of all these factors can effectively harm your lungs if you aren't careful.

Shorten your lifespan

You must have heard that happy people tend to live longer. Well, this is true because those who experience high levels of stress tend to have shorter lives. Experiencing constant stress and anger can effectively shorten your lifespan according to a study. If you are uncomfortable about expressing your emotions, especially powerful ones like anger, then it can have a negative effect on your overall well-being.

The Inability to Express Anger

Some people don't seem to think that anger is problematic. Whenever something frustrating happens, they can handle their feelings without suppressing them or having an angry outburst. However, not everyone feels comfortable with their anger. Most of us tend to suppress our anger because society has conditioned us to believe that anger is a negative and undesirable emotion. Ignoring a powerful emotion like anger is unhealthy.

When you ignore your anger, you tend to create an internal imbalance of emotions and face an internal struggle that others are unaware of. You might look fine on the outside, but you might feel like you are being disrespected, ignored, or even feel like your emotions don't matter. You might be stopping yourself from speaking up because you don't want any confrontation.

You might disguise anger by using indirect comments or might even opt for sarcasm as a means to express your anger. All these things essentially mean the same thing — you are suppressing your anger. Suppressing your anger is almost as bad as being unable to control your anger. In this section, you will learn about the ways in which anger can hurt you when you leave it unexpressed.

Impact on communication

The natural reaction triggered by anger tends to affect your ability to understand what is being said accurately. A lot of fights or arguments tend to escalate because people react based on what they think is said instead of what is said. Passive anger or anger which isn't expressed actively tends to break free in ways you cannot anticipate like pretending that things are fine when they aren't or agreeing even when you want to disagree. People seem to think that they can avoid any troubles by ignoring their anger. Well, this doesn't work, and suppressing anger will only lead to the formation of resentment and more anger.

Affects your health

As discussed in the previous section, anger tends to have an impact on your overall health. Well, the same stands true for unexpressed anger. Suppressing anger can lead to an increase in the risk of heart disease and strokes, weakens your immune system, increases anxiety, and can even shorten your lifespan. Repressing anger leads to several harmful physical manifestations, which affect your quality of life.

Impact on your emotions

You cannot manage your emotions without identifying them. For instance, you tend to feel fear in your stomach, anger in your head or upper body, whereas you experience heaviness in your heart when you are sad. Once you identify the emotion, you are experiencing. The next step is to accept it without any judgment. You cannot classify feelings as either good or bad, because they are a natural part of life. You require practice and show some self-love if you want to identify emotions. You increase your risk of dependency as well as addictions if you avoid or suppress your feelings. You might unknowingly develop certain compulsive behaviors to cope with any repressed emotions. Instead of doing all this and harming your mental and emotional well-being, it is better to recognize and accept your emotions.

Effect on values

The longer you suppress your anger, the more difficult it is to regain control of that anger. Anger is a powerful emotion which can turn even the most mild-mannered person into someone quite aggressive. Denying or suppressing your anger causes it to leak out in unanticipated ways, and this can cause more harm than you ever thought was possible. Your anger can get the best of you, and it can have a negative impact on your values. Did you ever notice that when your anger explodes, you tend to become extremely critical of others and perhaps say or do things that you normally wouldn't? Well, this is one of the reasons why suppressing anger is a bad idea.

Effect on trust

Anger can create a false image. You might say that everything is fine, but your behavior says otherwise. All those who like to please others tend to gain the approval of others by avoiding conflict. So, this tends to create a pattern of codependency. Pretending that things are fine even when they will create problems. If you never express your anger in front of your family or friends and on one fine day you have an angry outburst, then the way others view you will change. Denying your emotions will only create a lot of confusion and trust issues in a relationship. Trust is one of the pillars of a healthy relationship. So, if you aren't your authentic self, it will certainly cause problems in the future.

Please remember that emotions are temporary, so ignoring them is a bad idea. Don't repress your emotions. Instead, you must take steps to learn to control your emotions.

About Anger Management

Anger management is a process that helps you identify your anger triggers or stressors. It essentially provides you simple steps that you can use to manage your anger and stay calm even in frustrating situations. It helps you decrease the chances for any angry outbursts. It is impossible to avoid certain anger triggers; however, anger can be controlled. You can learn to respond calmly instead of reacting harshly when your anger is triggered. Anger management is not a new concept, and it dates back to thousands of years. Some of the famous philosophers like Francis of Assisi, Aelius Galenus, and Lucius Seneca all highlighted the need for adjusting one's perspective to lead happy lives. Their philosophies also talk about the need to avoid any such situations that incite anger. Some of the prominent modern-day anger management gurus include Louis Dundin, Peter Stearns, Howard Kassinove, and Raymond Novaco.

Anger management provides certain guidelines that give an individual a chance to handle their anger and express it in a constructive manner. It encourages people to examine their anger triggers and devise the appropriate response to those triggers in the future. Anger management strategies encourage individuals to identify their usual emotional reaction to any given situation and make any necessary changes to prevent anger from getting the best of them.

Benefits of Anger Management

Anger management strives to reduce and manage the emotional and physiological triggers, which incite anger. At times, you cannot get rid of change or avoid certain things, people, or circumstances which trigger your anger, but you can certainly control the way you react. One thing you will always have absolute control over regardless of the circumstances is the way you choose to respond. In this section, you will learn about the different benefits that anger management offers.

Empathy quotient

Anger management helps improve your empathy toward others, and in turn, this helps you understand other people's perspective. Usually, anger tends to escalate because people fail to see a situation from the perspective of the other person. Once you start becoming more empathetic, instead of thinking about everything from your perspective, you become more considerate towards other people's perspectives too. If you can do this, then it reduces the chances of a conflict. Also, empathy is a brilliant trait, which will come in handy in all aspects of your life.

Better relationships

Usually, most people tend to avoid their loved ones when they realize that their anger can hurt others. Since your closest circle consists of people you love, they often become the unintended victims of your angry outbursts. By learning to control your emotions, it makes it easier to develop healthier and happier relationships.

Gives insight

Anger management gives you a chance to learn about your anger its triggers, and its causes. The way that you feel and behave is directly related to what you feel and experience. By becoming aware of your emotions, you can easily understand what prompts them. For instance, you might realize that your anger is usually because of some repressed guilt or sadness you feel. Often, anger cloaks certain underlying emotions. So, anger management gives you an insight into your feelings and emotions. Once you understand all this, it certainly becomes easier to control and manage your anger.

Better judgment

Does a fight with your loved one make it difficult to concentrate on your work? Well, anger can cloud your judgment. When you are angry, rational and logical thoughts tend to go out of the window, and instead, anger tends to govern the way you react and behave. When your anger is under control and you are calm, you can think clearly and make better decisions. Anger management will help control your emotions, and this, in turn, will improve your decision-making skills.

Less stress

A significant benefit of anger management is the ability to manage stress. When your stress levels decrease, you will notice that it becomes easier to avoid any anger triggers and stay in control of any situation. Less stress also means better health. Apart from this, it improves your efficiency and productivity. So, by learning to manage your anger, you can effectively reduce your stress levels.

Avoid aggressive communication

Anger is quite a powerful emotion, and it often triggers aggression. If you can communicate effectively and efficiently, then you can easily avoid any angry outbursts. A lot of problems can be solved rather easily if you can communicate efficiently. By communicating this way, you can reduce the chances of miscommunication and express yourself clearly. Instead of responding aggressively, when you learn to manage your anger, you will be able to assert yourself in a proper manner. Anger management will help you understand that you can effectively assert yourself without resorting to aggression.

Understand your responsibility

Anger management will help you understand and recognize the ways you are responsible for your anger. It helps you become aware of your anger, along with the reasons for it. A combination of these factors will help regulate and manage your anger.

Now that you are aware of all the different benefits of anger management, it is time to learn more about the steps involved in this process.

Chapter 5. Using Psychology to Treat Anger

This is how you can use psychology to treat anger. Following these steps will help you regain your power rather than losing it because you have allowed violence to spin out of your control.

When angry, stand right where you are and look up and to the side. By doing this, your mind to switches attention from your feelings or your current state of anger towards a physical object. Rather than allowing yourself to lower your gaze, focus on the things that are above you and take a deep breathe.

Slowly begin to count one to ten. According to research, there is evidence that shows this as a classic way of letting everything sink in and anger to cool down. There are mainly two significant ways in which you can do this. First, you can count 1 through to 10 by yourself from inside. Secondly, you can do this out loud.

If you are saying it aloud, there is a high chance that the people around you will know of this method of anger management. When they understand that, there is a chance that they will begin to smile silently. And as you see a smile triggers another smile and hence allowing you to calm down.

Slowly get up from your position and exhale the air from your lungs. The most important thing that you have to bear in mind about exhalation is that rumblings often accompany it. This way, you will begin to feel a relieve. It is like a heavy weight lifted off your shoulders. And you can now breathe normally once more.

Now, change the expression on your face. When angry, you will find that you begin to frown, bite your lower lip among other facial expressions demonstrating anger. In other words, it is our facial expression that mirrors our true inner feelings and emotions. By changing this expression, you can trigger the mind to turn the impact anger might have on your actions.

Jump up and down for some times. You can also choose to take a sit. You could also employ your favorite dance move that ultimately diverts you to a good mood. It could remind you of something funny that you have done in the past. These variations play a critical role in helping you cope with anger.

Take your hands to your neck and give yourself a message. This is one of the best ways in which you can boost the flow of blood in the body and especially to the brain. This, in turn, supplies adequate amounts of oxygen to the brain and this has been shown to have a calming effect.

Allow your eyes to wander out the window. Out there, nature is beautiful. Look at the flowers, the weather and the people moving up and down chatting away in happiness. Being able to appreciate how things are still moving on even when you are upset helps you understand that very moment and the fact that you deserve happiness no matter what is going on around you.

Is there a way that you can change the situation? Admittedly, there is nothing permanent other than death. This means that, even though things may not have happened according to your expectations, it is not the end of the world. There are many ways of killing a rat. Rather than stirring up anger feelings, change your focus to identifying an alternative solution to the problem. This gives your mind something to work with other than getting carried away by anger.

Remember that it is another person with their desires, goals, and feelings. Many time, we tell ourselves that we are not the cause of the anger we have because of it someone else's fault. We then overreact and allow violence to boil over. But the truth is, it is worth waiting for another person's reaction to get and keeping our cool rather than the other way around.

Sometimes, the best way in which you can change a situation is to explain the reason why you are feeling that way. Well, it is true that this should not be done when you are burning in anger. But rather than getting so mad at someone, remember the good things they have done before.

When you do that, you are allowing anger to subside. In other words, when you learn how to manage your passion effectively, you avoid putting yourself in situations that will cause your anger and fury portray you as a monster. If there are other ways in which you can keep your cool, then now is the times to train yourself for when that moment comes.

Attending anger management classes

One of the best things with attending an anger management class is the fact that it helps you focus on expressing your anger, rage, and frustrations in class so that you can better understand the main factors that trigger your feelings of anger and hence, learn how you can cope when in such situations. In anger management classes, you will be able to cover specific scenarios that range from anger in public to anger at home, in your relationships as well as at the workplace.

With this, you will be exposed to a more coordinated programme that will require you to participate in a surrounding that is safe and supportive entirely. You have to appreciate the fact that treatment comprises or the ability to promote healthy behaviors that will help you cope with the situation at hand while ensuring that you develop excellent interpersonal communication skills that will help you appreciate others and their opinions. This is precisely what will help you constructively manage communications.

The good thing with a Priory is the fact that they fully understand that 'one-size-fits-all' kind of approach does not always work when it comes to anger management treatment. This means that they will treat your situation as unique so that you get the help that you need once they have conducted a careful and more personalized assessment.

Chapter 6. Mental Health and Anger

Anger is not always a disorder by itself. Sometimes, it can signify another mental disorder. When assessing anger, a therapist should address any underlying diagnosis; there are a number of mental conditions closely linked to anger including:

- Oppositional Defiant Behavior - hostile or angry behavior is one of the major signs of ODD in children.
- Post-traumatic stress disorder - PTSD often leads to an outburst of anger even without provocation. The stress pushes a person to the edge such that the mind stops functioning normally.
- Bipolar - One common feature of mania is irritability. A person may have anger symptoms in the depressive phase.
- Major depression - anger may be directed at self or others
- Narcissistic personality - A narcissistic person may lash out in anger if someone hurts or attacks his/her ego. They use anger to mask other feelings such as fear and inferiority.

The connection between stress and anger

(the role of stress in anger and the role of anger in stress)

You might ask yourself if stress is the same as anger. Is stress a result of anger or is anger a result of stress? People say that there is more anger in the world today than 20 years ago. Considering the current living conditions, this might be true. Other people say that there is more anger today and it is evident in workplace violence, road rage, school shootouts, et cetera. Stress can increase certain problems and if you experience anger often, chances are, stress will make it worse.

Healthy stress is very good when controlled. Eustress (Healthy stress) makes us get out of bed in the morning and pursue our dreams. It is also the thing that makes us stay attentive throughout the day. This type of stress does not lead to irritability or anger. The people lacking Eustress are normally referred to as unmotivated or lazy by others.

There are substances that can increase anger and stress including sugar, caffeine, nicotine, and excess food. There are also substances and practices that can help to reduce stress including exercises, learning communication, hobbies, journaling, yoga, deep breathing, Qigong, and engaging in social activities.

Quick tips for managing stress and anger

- Ask yourself "will it matter tomorrow, next week or next month?"
- Understand that the only person responsible for you is yourself.
- Understand that anger and stress is energy. It is up to you to decide the way you want to use it; positively or negatively.
- Understand that if you allow other people to stress you, you are giving them the power to control you. Do you really want other people to manage your feelings?

The effect of stress and anger

Ideally, we should be in a state of homeostasis - balanced feeling and living. Physically, everything should be working perfectly and so should the emotions. There should be a full state of wellbeing, with no stress, anguish or anger. However, many things happen, upsetting that balance thus sending us into other states of existence. The dangers of the outside world are the leading cause of imbalances. An author and blogger called Robert M. Sapolsky, MD states that zebras do not get ulcers. In his book called "Why, Zebras Don't Get Ulcers," Dr. Sapolsky, states that when a zebra gets threatened by a predator, its alert senses rise. The blood pressure increases, adrenaline flow intensifies, and the animal gets into the fight or flight mode. Blood rushes to the legs and the heart; thus the zebra runs very fast. The zebra will either escape or die but either way, it forgets as soon as the situation has ended. However, that does not apply to humans.

Your beliefs and anger

As we have seen, there are a variety of reasons why one can get angry. Did you know or even suspect that the belief system of a person can cause a whole bout of anger? Researchers have found that a person's beliefs affect their anger levels. What do you believe in? Which beliefs do you hold dear? Which ones do you have yet they no longer serve you? Which ones are bringing you harm? By definition, a belief is something that you take as truth; therefore, hold onto it. It can be a list of dos and don'ts - a values system. For instance, you can believe that being a good person will get through life, you will always get your way, everyone should be kind at all circumstances, and that no one will take advantage of you. How true is that belief?

Many beliefs are formed during childhood based on what one is taught or what he/she has observed. The beliefs are often instilled by parents, guardians, teachers, or other authority figures. In many cases, these teachings are an asset when used well. However, some of them become beliefs that result in problems later in life. For instance, the people who are lead to believe that they should always have their way are substantially angrier than those who were taught that they could not win all the time.

The Iceberg

Anger is what we normally see. When a person is angry, we can see the signs, the physical changes inform us. Some people will sweat, others will clench fists and others will raise their voices. When you check closely, anger is actually the iceberg. What we all see is just the tip. There is a complex feeling behind the symptomatic, and it varies from one person to the other. The real iceberg can be made up of insecurities, fear, hurt pride, and frustration, feeling disrespected and other emotions.

Because the anger we see is just the iceberg, it takes some through detective work to identify the real cause. One has to identify the underlying issue, in order to help the angry person. The first step to controlling anger is to ask yourself, "what is causing these emotions?" "What makes me feel this way?" When a person examines the feelings and the causes of anger, then he/she can address the problem. Basic techniques such as breathing, counting, and meditating will help you deal with the tip of the iceberg in the short term, but more will be required for long term solutions.

Understanding the iceberg is a great way to control your own anger and that of other people. When you use the iceberg theory to analyze anger, it will be easy for you to understand the anger of another person. For instance, when a coworker is getting angry at work because of a reason that is minute, you will be able to see that there is another thing behind the current emotion. It is hard for you to reciprocate anger with anger when you know that they are acting out of fear, jealousy, insecurity, hurt, or past things. When we understand this, it is easier to be gentle in our reactions and empathic.

Alcohol, Drug Abuse, and Anger

Remember that the anger we see in people and in ourselves is just the tip of the iceberg. There is more to it. Some people will have anger management issues stemming from drug and substance abuse. Others have anger issues because of brain damage. In events where a person is abusing drugs and has anger management issues, the main problem is that the drugs are attacking the functionality of the brain. The more one uses drugs, the angrier he/she become. A variety of reasons can contribute to such anger. For instance, when the person runs out of drugs, he/she will get angry. If there are family or personal issues arising due to the drugs, and the affected person is unable to manage them, he/she will be angry. Direct chemical attacks on the brain can result in anger.

Note that, it is usually difficult to manage anger if the angry person uses drugs frequently. A therapist can work with such a person until he/she runs out of breath, and it will probably not work. Such people need help with substance abuse before they can work on anger. A substance abuse program will help the patient more than a direct anger management program.

Some people have anger problems because of brain injuries. The sections of the brain responsible for controlling anger and other impulses are referred to as frontal lobes, and they are located right behind the forehead. An accident such as a car crash, hitting your head or falling can turn an otherwise calm person into an enraged and angry individual. Actually, it is very easy to damage the brain to the extent where you keep losing your temper. In the event that an angry person once had an accident that might have damaged the brain, it is advisable for him/her to visit a neurologist before engaging an anger management therapist. There are medical interventions for some of these cases. They help a person before he/she can go for therapy. Most of the cases involving brain injury require one to combine psychiatric drugs with anger management programs. Although many people believe there is no hope for people with anger issues resulting from brain injuries, there is some help. A large number of people have learned to manage anger in spite of injuries. However, it takes a lot of dedication and work.

Chapter 7. Anger Counseling

Outrage is a secondary and confounding emotion. As a secondary emotion, anger can have various causes. Passion is established in dread: the dread of the obscure, fear of disappointment and any number of different feelings of dread one may have. Terror is the essential emotion to which outrage is appended. Anger is not an awful emotion; however, it comes to the heart of the matter of outrageous or a wild point; it is presumably time to look for help.

How would you know whether your outrage is wild? If your anger:

- is distancing you from others, particularly your friends and family,
- has demolished or is destroying your connections,
- has to lead or is driving you to physically and emotionally harmed others,
- has to lead or is forcing you to be a social and legitimate inconvenience,

is the most significant supporter of your grief, or

Makes you deny you have an issue with it. At that point, your outrage is something other than an emotion, and it is an unmanageable issue. Living in resentment is the poor quality of life and no chance to get in which different people who adore you need to see you live. Luckily, there are approaches to manage outrage issues profitably through advising.

Outrage advising re-shows the mind to respond reasonably to possibly dangerous circumstances. An annoyance counselor energizes positive self-talk and self-assessment, talking and assessing oneself usually to overcome a situation in which outrage emerges. Different methods presented in annoyance directing may include:

- instructing oneself to require some investment outs to diffuse a displeasure actuating circumstance,

- taking part in physical exercise to discharge endorphins,
- actualizing unwinding systems, for example, profound breathing or yoga,
- utilizing diversion to diffuse hazardous conditions, and

other ways of dealing with stress chose in the advising procedure.

Outrage does not need to control you or your life. If your annoyance is controlling you or getting to be unmanageable, the time has come to get help. Living in annoyance harms you, yet everyone around you. It doesn't need to hurt. Outrage can be a gainful and helpful emotion when taken care of accurately. Discover how to utilize your annoyance and dread to enable you to carry on with a superior life as opposed to giving it a chance to use you.

Control Your Anger with Anger Counseling

How about we face a few actualities - life will dependably have times of pressure. Due dates at work; budgetary issues at home; coldblooded drivers on the turnpike; inconsiderate laborers at the store - on some random day, numerous sorts of components can combine and make you have an inclination that you need to shout. In any case, indeed a few people can serenely deal with their ordinary disturbances and burdens, while others aren't.

Even though outrage is a consummately normal emotional reaction to certain everyday circumstances, any furious sentiments that are left unchecked can harm connections just as one's close to home wellbeing. Outrage, the board, can be thought of like the way toward controlling your emotional sentiments only as of the physical reactions to those emotions, including raised circulatory strain and an expanded dimension of adrenaline. For specific individuals, managing their annoyance can be similarly as simple as strolling into another space to unwind, or taking a full breath and tallying to ten. For different people, making a fit of anger, the board class might be the best arrangement.

Notwithstanding the sort of individual, you are, the principal determinant to your prosperity is you! If you are not willing to take an interest in a class, at that point the majority of the anger directing on the planet won't help you by any stretch of the imagination. If you need to figure out how to adapt to your resentment flare-ups and restrained irate emotions, at that point just through being completely open with others would you be able to guarantee that you will effectively total treatment?

Finding outrage the executive's treatment isn't troublesome, because there are without a doubt many gathering treatment classes accessible everywhere (even free courses). The free ones won't more often than not be promoted, because of the humiliation it might cause for a portion of the general population who go to these sessions. When you look on the web, there is a decent shot that you can locate a couple of areas where these sorts of classes are being held. Your family specialist may likewise have the capacity to prescribe a spot you can go to.

Outrage Management Counseling

Every individual encounter outrage on different occasions for the duration of their lives, and this is splendidly typical. Anger the executives directing usually is just vital when somebody is crazy and allows their annoyance to control their activities. Outrage is an emotion that can fluctuate in degree; from being irritated to spiraling wild into attacks of fierceness. It isn't the way that we have anger that is the main problem, and it's how we manage outrage in our lives that decides whether outrage is an issue. At the point when scandal begins controlling how individual demonstrations or acts, and after that drives this individual to end up savage or forceful, outrage directing ought to be considered.

At the point when left unchecked and uncontrolled, outrage can prompt serious issues in each part of an individual's life, including connections, and here and there even constitutional issues. Scandal the board guiding can help keep somebody from accomplishing something cruel and reckless that they generally wouldn't have done. It's smarter to get guiding than to plan something unalterable for somebody you cherish and need to live with it for an incredible reminder. A ton of times individuals with indignation issues feels like they are vulnerable and there's nothing they can do to gain power. With annoyance the board advising they can oversee this incredibly ground-breaking emotion known as displeasure.

Much the same as bliss, bitterness, and jealousy, and love, outrage is an emotion that can be communicated in a wide range of ways. Changes in the body happen when somebody encounters and passion. They are both organic and physiological commonly, and effects affect the body. Generally, they incorporate an expanded pulse that is brought about by an expansion in adrenaline. If somebody is crazy, which means they can't control their reaction to these changes, the normal response of their body dominates. If they have a natural inclination to turned out to be loaded up with wrath and threatening vibe while encountering outrage, their body indeed dominates, and there is nothing they can do about it. A few people even dark out when they become excessively angry and go into wrath or anger, winding up savage and sinister, and they don't recall a thing. Outrage the executives advising is unquestionably essential if this happens.

There are numerous signs that an individual show when they are crazy with regards to outrage. They frequently lash out at the individual or individuals who have made them turned out to be furious. Wild shouting or crying is regularly connected with resentment issues. Knee jolting is an automatic reaction to outrage. Here and there an individual that is chafed with resentment will have flushing skin, just as shaking or trembling. Likewise, when somebody is furious, they can make substantial mischief themselves as well as other people.

If you or anybody you know to experience any of these activities or reactions because of anger, it might be essential to look for annoyance the executives directing. There are no fast goals, yet with assistance and direction, outrage the executives is conceivable and can get you back in charge once more.

Anger Management for Kids for When Things Get Out of Hand

Children are generally not frank concerning sharing sentiments and emotions. A child could be troubled with feelings of agony and blame yet it is improbable that you will take in this from him in a discussion. A tyke will, in general, demonstrate his sentiments by his conduct. When he is tragic, a youngster will presumably remain independent from anyone else and not have a lot to state. At the point when liable, he keeps away from the organization of individuals and would stay in his room. At the point when a youngster needs outrage the board for children, they break their toys, shout as well as pitch fits. Kids are not always vocal in connection to what they are feeling, yet his activities will say what his words are most certainly not.

At the point when kids show outrage, by propelling off into attacks of the fierceness and tossing themselves about on the floor in fits of rage, he needs to experience the way toward realizing what outrage the board for children can instruct him. These activities are signed presents on a parent that this youngster needs assistance. When untreated, this issue could form into a sea brimming with future trouble. Outrage the executives for these youngsters is accessible, and it is successful in dealing with their problems with annoyance. Finding the best displeasure, the executive's assets for children calls for research and experimentation. Different assets give tips about the inconvenience the board to kids. There are motion pictures, books, and a lot of other accommodating data that can be found on sites on the web. If you are worried about a youngster who experiences difficulty concerning outrage, you should look at a portion of the available web assets.

Helping a kid handle his emotions may include unique projects that are focused on children. A tyke won't profit by a grown-up annoyance gathering, and they won't benefit by taking an outrage the board course. These suggestions while brilliant for grown-ups are unreasonably experienced for a kid. Their brains have not sufficiently grown for them to have the capacity to disclose their sentiments to other individuals yet. In all trustworthiness, they may not comprehend what is happening themselves. A counselor does not anticipate that a tyke should open up and educate him concerning his positive emotions which makes him furious. These subtleties are found through a scope of exercises that show outrage the board for children.

Children react well to activity exercises so including amusements in their treatment is probably going to be a savvy begin to outrage the executives for children. It is better than they are encouraged positive qualities and satisfactory conduct through the diversions than it would be for them to complete a one-on-one session with a counselor. When they are given worksheets, shading books, tests, and riddles the displeasure, the executives for children in a split second ends up fascinating and charming. At these occasions, kids could be taking an interest in a program and not understand it. Outrage, the executives, is a troublesome plan to disclose too little youngsters. Considering the way that youngsters are uninformed of their religious sentiments and are not prepared to think rapidly and support their choices, it is tough to encourage them successful exercise plans which require coherent reasoning.

Outrage, the board for children, is fundamental. A tyke needs to figure out how to act legitimately when in various circumstances. The must realize that it is consummately fine to be irate. However, they likewise need to comprehend that this outrage ought not to be utilized bad. Instructing youngsters anger the executive's aptitudes right off the bat in life will give building squares to their future. By rehashing exercises and practices, kids, in the long run, learn outrage the executives for children.

Concerning your children, however, if you need him communicating his resentment appropriately in under 48 hours, go to my site, I have free recordings that are stacked with data to that discloses to you progressively about it.

Anger Management for Kids

Outrage Management for Kids is more earnestly to deal with than at any other time since youngsters like to learn by watching others. What's more, today, as a result of the Internet, TV, PCs and computer games, there are many negative or sketchy icons that youngsters need to adjust with.

It's tough to show kids how to control and deal with their annoyance. First and the most vital assignment ought to look for the wellspring of the fierceness. The most severe issue happens when that equivalent source is something in the house.

Most clinician guarantee that finding the wellspring of annoyance is the ideal approach to begin controlling outrage of a tyke. Well established certainty is that the vast majority of kids don't realize how to control their resentment and express their emotions. Youngsters are entirely flighty, so one ought to get into their heads when attempting to manage their outrage.

To begin with, attempt to find the issue. Outrage the executive's systems for children won't tackle anything if you don't chip away at them. Discover genuine reason for annoyance. Obvious causes are single child rearing, absence of correspondence among guardians and tyke, divorces and so on. Try not to think like a grown-up when you are endeavoring to discover issues. Children see the world in a specific manner.

Furthermore, remember that counteractive action can stop all outrage issues. Talk, talk and chat with your tyke. Speak with your youngster on a similar dimension. Attempt to clarify them genuine issue.

Give them a wide range of points of view. Attempt to drive them to consider the matter and their conduct. Topics ought to be explained when tyke understands the wellspring of the issue. With consistent correspondence, you will most likely control your youngster's resentment and fierceness.

Anger Management for Children - 7 Tips That Will Work Today

The central inquiry that numerous guardians have with regards to child rearing is "How would I grow great outrage the executives for youngster's aptitudes?" And although there are a few approaches to taking care of an irate tyke who won't comply with their parent, these seven hints will come path in helping guardians gain the power they are urgently looking for.

1. Never show emotion - Showing emotion will add fuel to a hot flame. Youngsters can detect irate emotions from their folks, and consequently, they will prove considerably more resentment.

2. Realize your outrage triggers- - What is it your inclination directly before you have an angry tirade with your youngster? It's critical to realize your tipping focuses.

3. Acknowledge what's your shortcoming - Parents who acknowledge obligation regarding the battles that happen in their house are bound to defeat the circumstance since they can concoct arrangements on the most proficient method to address it.

4. R.e.l.a.x- - Parents who practice unwinding methods are rationally arranged to manage undesirable fiendish practices that youngsters show. The way that they aren't effectively enraged will have a quieting impact on the tyke who urgently need positive results.

5. Look for arrangements - Parents who look for answers for displeasure the executives for kids will more often than not discover them. This might be expert advice, or it might be as a child-rearing help gathering.

6. Get familiar with the specialty of exchange - Parents who understand that to get what they need, that they should quit any pretense of something, realizes how to get their children to react decidedly.

7. Overlook offensive conduct - If your child's behavior is a reoccurring issue, it is because they have discovered that their terrible behavior stands out enough to be noticed. When the action isn't hazardous, overlook it. Your tyke will find that the conduct isn't working.

Outrage the executives for youngsters isn't instructed in the present high schools, so tragically guardians understand that they need preparing in this imperative zone when the issue is a 55lb, crying, hollering, gnawing kid who will not return the Hershey's sweet treat. With tolerance and a longing to learn, guardians are furnishing themselves with the information they have to reestablish request.

Chapter 8. How To Get To The Root Of Your Anger

Sometimes, your anger might be rooted in self-esteem issues that you might not even be aware of. The anger might be a way of masking these problems. Other times, your anger might be rooted in painful memories about something that happened to you in the past, perhaps even during your childhood. In this case, your anger could be your brain's way of automatically distracting you from this pain. It gives you a sense of control over your vulnerability and fear. Anger essentially tells us that something is wrong, though it does not necessarily what that is. Unfortunately, anger spurs us to take action, which means that sometimes we might take action without even knowing what the real issue is.

The first step to dealing with anger is to ask yourself an important question: why are you so angry? Only by answering this question and uncovering the actual reason behind your anger will you be able to effectively deal with it. Sometimes, getting to the actual reasons behind your anger might need a lot of time and a lot of digging. However, without uncovering the underlying issues behind your anger, trying to address your anger problem will be like treating the symptoms while doing nothing about the actual illness.

Recognize That You Are Getting Angry

In order to know to get to the root of your anger problem, you need to learn to recognize when you start getting angry. Many people with an anger problem might not even notice when their anger starts rising. They only notice it once it is already boiling and getting out of control. So, the first thing you need to do is to take notice of your anger once it starts rising. Keenly observe it and watch how it progresses. For instance, your anger might start as anxiety before turning into an irritation and then progressing to frustration and morphing into full-blown anger. Following your anger as it progresses through all these emotions will make it easier for you to identify the emotions that often precede your anger, which might in turn point you to the underlying issue.

Identify Your Anger Triggers

You should try to identify the specific thoughts or incidents that trigger your anger. If you frequently get angry, you might recognize that there are certain thoughts or incidents that seem to trigger your anger more often. The triggers that frequently trigger your anger might point to one of the three major causes of anger – fear, frustration, or pain. For instance, if your anger is frequently triggered by things such as your friends showing up late or canceling plans, your kids not making their beds, bad traffic, and so on, this shows that the frustration of things not as you expect is the main reason behind your anger problem. From there, you can focus on trying to find out why you get easily frustrated. Similarly, if your anger is frequently triggered by things such as your partner staying out late, the fear of abandonment could be the major reason behind your anger problem.

Sometimes, you might notice that you tend to get angry when you are in a particular environment. For instance, you might notice that you rarely get angry at home, but your irritability seems to be exceptionally high at work. This can be a pointer that you are working in a stress-filled environment which could be the reason behind your anger problem, rather than something about you. In this case, finding another job can help you reduce your likelihood of getting angry.

Keep An Anger Journal

Keeping an anger journal is an effective way of understanding your anger and the reasons behind it. An anger journal is simply a book where you keep a record of your outbursts of anger. Every time you go through a moment of anger, get your journal and record the situation. You should really look deep into yourself and be very honest with yourself when doing this. Write down the incident that triggered your anger, what was happening at that moment, how you were feeling right before it happened, the signs of anger that you felt in your body, the thoughts that accompanied your anger, the intensity of your anger, what you did in reaction to your anger, how other people reacted to your anger, how long you were angry for, how you felt after the anger subsided, whether the issue was resolved or not and so on.

Keeping an anger journal helps you understand the kind of situations and incidents that trigger your anger, your reactions to anger, the thoughts and emotions that accompany your anger and so on. This can give you important clues that will help you uncover any underlying issue behind your anger. When writing your anger journal, it is important to be very detailed. Include each and every little thing pertaining to your anger. In addition, you should avoid judging your feelings when writing your anger journal. The aim here is to gain awareness of your emotions, which will in turn make it easier for you to understand the issues behind the emotions.

Dig Deep by Asking Why

People often have a problem getting to the root of their anger because they only look at it superficially. They don't take the time to dig deeper and question their anger. For instance, if you find yourself upset because your spouse stayed out late, you might tell yourself that you are angry because he stayed out late, which is wrong according to you. However, many will not dig deeper to understand why they think a spouse staying out late is wrong. In order to uncover this, you need to ask yourself several consecutive 'whys. Below is an example of how you might do this:

I feel so angry right now. Why? Because my husband stayed out late. Why did this offend me? Because I don't know what he was doing out there. Why does this bother me? Because my ex-boyfriend cheated on me, and I am afraid of being cheated on again.

In this case, the endless trail of questions can help you uncover the fact that you are not angry because your husband stayed out late, but because you are afraid of being cheated on again. By digging deeper, you gain more insights about your anger and get to the root of the issues behind your anger. From there, you can focus on addressing the issue rather than the feeling.

Distinguish Between Real And Imagined Anger

Sometimes, the trigger behind your anger is usually a very minor incident. However, your imagination might blow up the incident and trigger an angry reaction that is not proportional to the incident behind the anger. For instance, let's assume you are on your way to work in the morning, and you find that there has been an accident that has resulted in a huge traffic snarl up. Since you expected to get to work early, you will naturally feel some annoyance and frustration because of the traffic. However, there is not much you can do about it, and ideally, you would accept the situation and your frustration would subside quickly.

Unfortunately, this is not what happens in most situations. Instead of accepting the situation, your imagination takes over and starts conjuring worst-case scenarios of what might happen because of the traffic snarl up. You imagine meeting your boss on the elevator as you walk into work. You imagine not being able to finish the project you were working on in time for the presentation. You might think of the last time your boss yelled at a colleague forgetting to work late. You might even imagine being fired from your job because of your lateness.

By doing this, your imagination blows up the issue out of proportion. Instead of responding to the mild frustration of a traffic jam, your emotions respond to the imagined fear of getting fired from your job. You end up getting enraged and start cussing at the traffic jam. Even after the traffic eases, you continue feeling enraged because of the imagined scenarios playing out in your head.

One key to understanding your anger is to learn to distinguish between real and imagined anger. Whenever you find yourself feeling angry, take a moment to introspect and determine whether your anger is a response to a real situation or an imagined one.

Evaluate The Risk of Mental Health Problems

Sometimes, your anger problem might be result of an underlying psychiatric or psychological disorder. Anger is one of the symptoms of mental disorders such as dissociative identity disorder, obsessive-compulsive disorder, bipolar disorder, and so on. If you find yourself constantly overwhelmed by feelings of anger but you cannot pinpoint any possible reason behind your anger, this could be a sign that there is an underlying medical problem behind your anger. While the possibility of your anger being a result of a medical issue is a lot lower than having an anger management problem, it is better to be sure than sorry. If you are chronically angry without any clue as to why you are constantly feeling angry, it is wise to seek medical or professional opinion to determine whether there is an underlying condition.

- ●_It is important to get to the root of your anger problem in order for you to address the real issue instead of addressing feelings, which are only the symptoms of the problem.
- ●_The first step to understanding your anger is to learn to recognize when you are getting angry and follow the progression of your anger, instead of just taking note of the anger once it has already exploded.
- ●_Keeping an anger journal is also a great way of understand your anger, its triggers, your reactions to it, and the thoughts and emotions that accompany it.
- ●_Asking yourself a series of 'whys' can help you dig deeper and uncover the actual fear or pain behind your anger.
- ●_Sometimes, your anger is a response not to real situations, but to imagined situations created by your mind. Learn to distinguish between real and imagined anger.

- ● Sometimes, anger might also be a result of an underlying medical condition. If you are chronically angry without any clue as to why you are constantly feeling angry, it might be a good idea to seek the advice of a professional.

Chapter 9. Positive Self-Talk

This is a system used by psychiatrists and one that works well. When you feel that your mind is telling you something that makes you angry, counter it. Tell yourself something positive. The subconscious connection kicks in once again and your subconscious records the way you react to things. Thus, if you don't react as predicted, then you rewrite the information in your subconscious and override your usual way of dealing with things. Let's take a look at Ken and the way he dealt with his problems in his relationship. These are the thoughts that he had.

"How can I be expected to come home from work and then deal with the temper tantrum of my teen?"

This was the initial thought. Then it would build up. He would tell himself all about the trouble the teen was in. He would make the problem so huge that when he eventually got home, his anger was at such a pitch that he was sorely tempted to throw the teen out of the house. His wife knew that Ken loved his children. She also knew that the teen was pushing his luck. He had been smoking pot and he had been caught driving a car without permission. She expected Ken to lose his temper but, of course, no one really wins when that happens. The child gets afraid but rebels more because that's what kids do. The teen is getting to the age when he feels grown up, though we all know that this is a very indecisive time for kids. They are going through hormone changes. They are going through learning about bad relationships. It's a tough time for kids. Ken knew this but he still wasn't getting anywhere with the way that his mind was thinking. The kid could do nothing right and there was a love/hate relationship going through his mind that was tearing his emotions to pieces.

What Ken did, after being instructed, was that every time he thought a bad thought about his teen, he made himself respond to it with a positive thought. Thus, he was able to take moments from the child's life and use these to instill positive thoughts.

"The kid and I had great times when he were little and we should have great times again."

"The kid is a great kid and I love him very much."

Ken explained that while this did not make the problems go away, he tried very hard to remember all the good things about his teen and work on those rather than emphasizing the negative and making his teen pull even further away from him. The kid expected his father's anger, but instead, Ken responded with love and understanding. Ken taught his teen that sometimes kids make mistakes and that he was a bit worried about how this would affect him getting a job. Ken also explained that replacing negative with positive made him very aware of his own weaknesses and he didn't want his teen to inherit those weaknesses and see temper as the only way to deal with things. Calm talk and acceptance that his child was older worked well in his favor and he was able to talk his teen into becoming reasonable, apologizing for the mistakes he had made and realizing that his father was actually a good guy and a great example to him.

In Ken's case, he said that it also taught him his own weaknesses with emotions. He had never really been that demonstrative of his pride in his son, or his love for his son. He had gradually grown distant from the child because while the child was growing into an adult, Ken had very little time with him and thus missed out on all the mistakes and all the good things too. He found himself crying one night into his pillow because he realized that, had he continued to demonstrate anger toward his child, he would have lost him. There was absolutely no doubt in his mind about that. Thus, being able to replace angry thoughts with positive ones worked in many ways to help Ken to deal with his emotions.

People who have self-esteem issues always seem to talk negatively to themselves. They are unable to find the courage to be who they really are because they are too busy being who they tell themselves they are. Words like "I am useless" or "I am not capable of doing this" need to be replaced with positive affirmations that replace the negative. That's when you learn that it's not so much about what's happening in the world. It's more about how YOU handle it. When you begin to handle things in a better manner, you get better results. It's as simple as that.

Exercise in Self-Talk

Today is going to be a new start. Every negative thought is going to be replaced with a good thought. Thus, as soon as you think something negative, replace it with something positive. It really helps to mend the damage done by anger.

Practical Guide to Stay Positive

Hold on to a Positive Thought

We are all little rays of sunshine. Despite how off track our lives become, there are always moments in a day when we manage to muster enough courage to think of something positive. Now, the first stage (gathering positive thoughts) is easy. However, the difficult part is to hold on to them. It is important that whatever positive thoughts you think, you stick to them. Do not let happy thoughts wander by and get lost while you are busy in your daily life.

Allot Time

In order for this to happen, you must allocate time. You can call this Me-Time. Be it cooking, taking a break from studies, sitting in the office doing nothing or simply reading the newspaper in your front lawn, you can start collecting positive thoughts anywhere and anytime. Allocation of time ensures continuity and intensity.

The Glass is Half Full

Remember the evergreen question about whether the glass is half full or half empty? It all depends on how you see it. I would suggest you see it as half full. Being an optimistic is the best way to self-motivate. When you look at the brighter side of things, you naturally push yourself toward hope. Hope is a force that can win lost wars and topple tyrannical empires. Make sure you adopt a non-negative attitude towards life. Look for reasons to be happy in the smallest of things.

Address Not Avoid Negativity

There will be a lot of troubles in your lifetime; you cannot avoid them. What you can do to minimize their impact on you is address the negative aspects of it all. Remember to spot the silver lining of the cloud. A little bit of optimism goes a long way in deciding not just your present mood but also its impact on your overall productivity.

Set a Target

What is it that you are aiming for? Do you have an objective or a set of objectives in mind? Are you simply blindly aiming for an undecided target in the dark, groping for your bow and fumbling with your arrows? When you have a set target in mind, anger rarely finds the chance to take control of you. The motivation to achieve your aims in life keeps negative emotions at bay.

Motivate

In order to properly and efficiently motivate yourself, you need to first sit down and list all your goals. If you are taking a particular step, make sure you know its future course. Do not simply do something for the heck of it. Have a plan set in mind. The first step to all this is setting your goals. When you set your goals, you become aware of your direction. Everyone is supposed to be going in a specific direction. Have you found yours?

When you zero in on your direction, you have a purpose in life. This purpose will lead you to your goal. Your purpose could be to perform any immediate action that is supposed to lead you to your goal, thus achieving a greater success. The difference between goals and purpose is the difference between intention and motive. Your goal is to become rich; your purpose becomes doing business or hunting for a job. Goals, therefore, are a big set while purposes are their subsets.

Don't Be Directionless

A lot of anger finds its source from being directionless. Do not wander about aimlessly. You do more harm by roaming around directionless than by sitting idle doing nothing. Take your time but make sure you come up with your own set of goals. Your goals need not be long-term in nature. You could set your goals even on an hourly basis. All you need to take care of is that they should not be unrealistic, overtly ambitious or unachievable within the set time period and limited resource available at your disposal.

Get Your Priorities Straight

Anger also finds itself in places and people where there are no priorities. Most anger-related blunders happen due to people not being able to, first, have priorities, and second, set them in order. A pizza delivery guy's priority is reaching the destination within thirty minutes. If he does not adhere to the norm, he has to surrender the pizza for free, standing the chance of getting fired by his boss. We all have similar priorities to look after in life. If you fail to even recognize them, you are bound to fail.

Prepare a list of normal jobs like mowing the lawn, giving the car for a wash, or attending a really important office meeting. Having prepared such a list, you are now ready to prioritize.

Decide which jobs are absolutely necessary, which ones are mildly so and which ones can be rescheduled or neglected to return to later. Your decision should rest upon how much importance each job holds in your life.

Now think of each job as a little victory. Every time you finish a job, strike them off your list and move on to the next one.

Perform your day's work in this manner and you will never miss out on completing every task that has been scheduled or assigned.

Aim for Small Objectives

Instead of going out all guns blazing from the word go, you should try to conquer the small yet relevant victories. Winning is a practice and practice needs baby steps. These baby steps won't be possible if you have an intention to take gain leaps. Tread slowly and try to achieve less significant glories—the ones that require minimal effort and yet when achieved give maximum pleasure of having succeeded.

Do Not Hesitate to Fail

Remember, everything negative that happens to you happens for a reason. Life is full of lessons and there are different kinds of ways for you to learn them. One of the very effective ones is failing. When you fail, it hits you hard and you lay low for a while. You work on your game, train yourself harder and try to hit back stronger. This is how you gain motivation from failures. He who fails does not even attempt the dive. He is afraid he won't make it to the other side; he refuses to take the leap. However, if you use your failure as a lesson, this motivates you.

Look for Inspiration

Do not be ashamed to derive inspiration from those who have seen and done it all. We humans have always been dependent upon others—be it for food, shelter or inspiration, we have always derived them or inherited them from those who came before us. We have read books about great people who were down in the ditch and decided to take matters into their own hands to write history. Famous authors who are capable of creating vivid images in millions of minds, great world leaders who led nations to war and peace, awe-inspiring war heroes who defended boundaries with all they had—such people never fail to inspire others in their personal quests.

Chapter 10. Techniques To Calm You Down When You're Angry

It may seem like it's easy to lose your temper, lose control of your anger. You probably aren't even thinking about it when it happens. You just lose control. Even if you're aware it's happening, you just can't stop yourself.

If you're aware it's happening you can use a variety of techniques to regain control or stop yourself from losing control.

What Steps Can You Take to Calm You down When You're about to Lose Your Temper?

Close Your Eyes and Take a Breath

When you feel yourself getting angry, close your eyes? Take a deep breath.

Once you're arguing and getting angry your anger can become a self-realizing cycle: the angrier you feel the angrier you speak, the angrier you get. Sometimes we just need a pause in the fight to be able to take a step back and regain composure.

You're giving yourself a moment of reflection. Did we get off topic or let the argument get out of hand? Is the issue really worth raising my voice? Will I accomplish anything by getting angry?

You're calming yourself down. You're also sending the other person a visual message: I'm getting so angry I need to close my eyes a moment and take a breath. I'm angry. Do you want to continue like this, or should we both calm down or discuss it later?

Count to Ten

Stop talking and slowly count to ten or back to zero from ten.

Similar to closing your eyes and taking a breath when you stop and count you're doing several things.

You're stopping yourself from continuing to argue, giving yourself a moment to reflect and internally analyze the situation.

Once you stop arguing for a moment of quiet you'll begin to calm down, then you won't feel so angry.

You're telling the other person, I'm so angry right now I have to stop myself to count so I don't carry on and get angrier.

When they see how angry you are they'll reflect and analyze as well. They'll understand how angry you are, whether they want to continue arguing or resolve the issue or not.

Think about Something Else

Thinking about your "happy place" might be cliché, and you don't have to picture your happy place, but take your mind off your anger and the fight. Think about something else, whether it's a job you have to do later or what you're doing after work or what you're having for lunch or a mental image of some fun place you want to go to.

Take your mind off the fight for a minute, you'll stop fighting, and you'll realize you probably don't want to keep fighting.

The other person may notice you're distracted or mentally away and realize it's a good time to regain composure or postpone the discussion.

Explain You're about to Lose Your Temper

Stop fighting and simply tell the other person you're about to lose it.

People appreciate honesty. Is there a better time to be honest than just before you're about to blow up at someone?

They'll probably appreciate that you stopped and took the time to warn them before you blow up, and hopefully they'll think twice about continuing the argument.

Whether they do or not, they'll understand how serious it is to you, which may make them rethink their position at least a little, or consider a compromise more so than if you continued fighting and blew up at them.

Think about the Other Person

Try to stop and take a break from your stress and anxiety and put yourself in the other person's perspective.

If you're getting angry ask yourself, how do they feel?

They might be getting angry themselves. Why are they angry? What reasons would they have to get angry over the situation?

If they're not angry, why not? Why do they look calm or detached or sad rather than angry, or even maybe relieved? Maybe it's a situation they've wanted to talk to you about for some time, and finally they're getting the chance.

Look at it from their perspective. What's at stake for them? What could they lose or gain?

Maybe you can think of a compromise that works for both of you. If you can find one, you won't be angry anymore.

Avoid the Situation

If you're about to walk into a situation or discussion that you know will make you angry, try not to.

Ask yourself if it's something you don't have to deal with at this time. Can you put it off?

Are you about to talk to someone who always ruffles your feathers? Avoid them for now if you can. Try some of the previous techniques to keep your calm, and then deal with them.

Changes in a routine never hurt. Sometimes they can be invigorating.

If the clerk who always takes too long annoys you and makes you angry, go to another store, or wait for another clerk.

If the boss gave you a job you can't stand, work on something else for a little while if you can. Prepare yourself mentally, and then do the job.

When you avoid stress you can avoid anger. If you can't avoid it, try to put the most positive light on it you can. You hate the project, but the sooner you start, the sooner you'll finish. The clerk takes too long, but it gives you the opportunity to scan the store's stock or chat with another customer.

If you can't find a positive, try to focus on the issue, not the anger.

Focus on the Issue at Hand

Focus on the reason for the argument.

You didn't pick a fight with someone just to fight. (You did if you already lost control of your anger.)

Why did the argument start? What purpose did you have?

Focus on that. Concentrate on what you want to accomplish.

Remind yourself that getting angry probably won't help you accomplish your goal.

Work on the things that will accomplish your goal. Seeing the other person's perspective might be one way to do it, or at least find a suitable compromise.

What else can you do to reach your goal? Find another way to talk about the issue rather than getting angry and yelling or threatening.

Remind yourself of your goal and remind yourself that getting angry will take you further from it, not closer.

Watch Out for Triggers

Triggers are the things that make you react faster in anger: when your spouse rolls his eyes, when your boss gives you an order in a questioning tone, when your child whines and tugs your dress.

We all have triggers, and we all recognize them too. "So help me, if you sigh one more time...", "Stop tugging your hair!"

Recognize your triggers, warn yourself they're coming, and then tell yourself not to overreact to them.

The other person will stop soon. Remind yourself that if you don't lose your anger and blow up the trigger will pass, and you can get back to the issue at hand.

Walk away from a trigger if you need to.

Interrupt someone, politely, before they pull the trigger.

You might even explain to them that they're using a trigger and it's only going to make the situation worse. Try to explain it constructively, not destructively and not accusingly.

Try not to make statements like, "You only do that to annoy me."

If it's true, they know it without your stating it. If they've lost their anger too now you've confirmed the trigger works and they'll probably pull it.

If it's not true, you've accused them falsely, which is only going to exacerbate the problem and argument and cause you both to lose your anger even more.

Think Back to the Past

Stop a minute and think back on previous times you've gotten angry or lost your temper.

Try to remember what happened to make you angry. Was it the person you were talking to, or the issue you were discussing, or the location, or one trigger or another?

Look for patterns. We have routines and patterns every day. Were you fighting with your spouse over money, or your child about something dangerous they were doing, or a coworker about who has which responsibilities?

If you can recognize patterns that lead to making you angry, you can try to avoid them or change the pattern or routine.

Go back in your mind and picture previous times you got angry. Recognize the moment when you lost it. Analyze what happened. Who said what? What was the topic? What were your initial feelings?

Acknowledge the moment you lost it, look for it is coming in the present argument, and then steer away from it. Guide the discussion in another direction. Interact so the other person reacts differently and doesn't pull a trigger.

Remind yourself that you've come down this road too many times already in the past. There's no purpose to going down the same road again. You're only going to lead yourself to a worse fight and another unresolved conflict.

Walk Away

In most cases you can walk away from an argument, just walk away, especially if it's getting heated.

The other person knows its getting intense. They probably don't look forward to a fight any more than you do.

When you feel yourself getting angry, if you know it's a discussion that will end in a fight, walk away, until you've calmed down.

Until you resolve it, the issue's not going away. You can discuss it any time. Remind yourself that you might as well discuss it later when you're calm, rather than now when your temper's flaring.

If it's a discussion you can't avoid, find an excuse to leave, you've got to go to the bathroom; you just remembered an important call you have to make.

If you can't walk away, it's your job review or your spouse is between you and the door, either explain that you'd rather postpone it, or walk away in your mind. Think about something else. Most people realize when they're being tuned out and they'll end a conversation.

You can always return to it later if it's important, but you can't undo your temper after you've lost control of it and said or done something angry. Then all you can do is apologize and try to repair the damage.

How Can You Recognize When You're about to Lose It?

Angry isn't a normal state of being, not for most of us.

You can recognize physical and emotional signs that you're about to lose it.

Physical signs you're about to lose it:
- -Turning flush
- -Palms get sweaty
- -Heartbeat speeds
- -Breathe faster
- -Gritting your teeth
- -Speaking louder
- -Pacing
- -Tensing
- -Unable to sit still
- -Exaggerated gestures
- -Frowning
- -Angry expressions

You can have a wide variety of physical signs, recognizing them can help you to avoid getting angry, as well as recognizing emotional signs.

Emotional Signs You're about to Lose It:
- -Voice different than usual
- -Suddenly overly expressive
- -Exaggerated emotions
- -Overreaction
- -Quick to tears
- -Quick to anger
- -Thoughts becoming irrational

When you recognize when you're about to lose it you can try to stop yourself, calm yourself and retain control of your anger.

What Are the Best Ways to Handle Your Anger?

Whether you've lost it or maintained control try to direct or redirect your anger in constructive ways.

You can use various techniques for this:

Change your focus. If you're losing or lost your temper arguing one aspect of the issue, change the point you're arguing. Address another part of the issue.

You might find it's a part of the issue you can resolve easier. You can go back to the previous part later.

Ask for feedback. Ask the person you're arguing with how they feel. Explain how you feel, the feelings beneath your anger, whether you're scared or hurt or feel you're not being taken seriously.

Remind yourself of repercussions. Stop and try to imagine what will happen if you lose your temper before you lose your temper. Play it through to the end in your mind. The results probably won't be as productive as if you don't lose your temper.

Deflect your anger. Look for another emotive way to express your anger. Look for the comical in the situation or try to explain what would make you happy rather than what's making you angry.

Recognize when you're losing it. Keep an eye out for the signals that you're losing your temper. We all know when our blood's beginning to boil and we're going to lose it. If you can tell its coming you can use techniques to stop it from happening.

If you've gotten to the point where you lost control and you've insulted someone and even damaged a relationship, you can still do a few things to try to repair it:

Acceptance: Accept and acknowledge that you acted in destructive anger. Explain to the other person that you understand you lashed out without right and maybe even without cause.

Responsibility: When you accept and acknowledge you lost your temper, you should also take responsibility for it. No one's to blame but you. You might feel like the other person, or the situation pushed you to it, but you know that's not true. For any situation in our life there are a variety of reactions and behaviors we can have to it. Anger doesn't have to be the first.

Explain to the other person that you're taking responsibility. If they see you owning up to it they maybe be more inclined to work with you and repair damage.

Culpability: After taking responsibility you have to admit fault and acknowledge you need to make efforts to repair the damage.

Apologize: Apologize for losing your temper. No one doesn't like an apology, especially if you were wrong, and especially over a serious argument.

An apology can make a huge difference in whether they'll repair damage with you or not.

Amends: Beyond the apology if the other person is willing to work with you, find out what you can do, what they'd like you to do, to try to repair the damage.

Maybe they're satisfied with an apology. Maybe you owe them money. Maybe you still have to have a long talk about the issue or the past or the future.

You might still need to talk about the issue or issues that led to it even after you lose it. You need to regain composure.

Can You Regain Composure after You Lost It?

You can regain composure through a variety of techniques and strategies.

You may need to regain composure. The issue probably wasn't resolved after you lost it. You might have some apologizing to do too.

Calm down. It seems obvious, but it's hard to do after you lose your temper. You might need to take a walk or get out of that room or go do something else for a little while.

You should take some deep breaths. Go for coffee or tea.

Read the newspaper or surf online.

Do something to take your mind off what made you angry.

Revisit the discussion after you've calmed down.

Ask for sympathy. Weakness is strength. We're all vulnerable. Other people relate faster to vulnerability and weakness than they do to posturing and aggression.

Explain that you just got so angry that you lost it, and ask the other person to excuse you and even see your side of it.

Explain that you're embarrassed for losing it and you'll work not to the next time.

See other perspectives. Imagine you're the other person. What do they want? What do they have to gain or lose? Why is it so important to them to win? Could they settle on a compromise?

If you can see the other person's perspective, you can understand why you shouldn't have lost it. We all have a right to our wants and needs. They have as much right to seek them as you do. You don't have the right to lose it.

Even if they were clearly in the wrong, two wrongs don't make a right.

If you're quick to match a wrong with a wrong and lose your temper, you may have an anger management problem.

It's important to determine whether you do or not, because relationships can be on the line.

Meditation For Anger

Meditation is one of the most powerful practices you can use to manage any depression or anger you have inside. It can be the real cure for stresses in your life and by doing less, it can give you a stack of energy. I have used this practice in my own life every day for the past three years and have seen a massive change in how I approach problems and my overall happiness.

I'm one of those people who really struggle with becoming grounded especially when something happens that I can't control. I sometimes lose it and then look at the way I acted and feel disappointed but proud that I have the power to assess what happened. Most people get angry, and they won't be able to see where they went wrong, and they will blame it on a diagnosis. It's my anger problem not me. A lot of people look at meditation as something boring but if you can have an open mind about it, it's an extremely powerful practice.

All the major leaders in the world talk about how they meditate for 20 minutes every day just so they feel like they have control of their minds. People that don't relax themselves and shut their brain off often are more prone to getting angry and depressed. I have done plenty of research throughout my life with mediation and it's number one objective is for you to become present. If you are living in the moment, all your problems disappear, and it gives you a rest from the constant battle of life. If you feel like you can't create peace of mind in your life then this will help you create it fast.

I have talked to a lot of people in my life and the majority of them tell me that becoming present in the moment is really difficult, especially if you don't live there. I can guarantee if you want to switch your anger to happiness, you need to do things outside the box. You need to see what works for you by trying a number of things and you will be able to have life experience with them. That's what gives me power to talk my experience. I have been through anger management and I know exactly the kinds of thoughts and beliefs they have. This has worked for me. It doesn't necessarily mean it's going to work for you but I'm sure you will see some kind of change in behaviour.

Meditation is a practice that I took up because of my lack of presence with people and the shift that I have created in the last decade is amazing. Most people take meditation and just sit there hoping one day their anger will surpass. By not thinking and just feeling present and noticing the air on your skin or, the smells around you takes your focus off your problems. Negative problems put so much stress on yourself that it constantly makes you overthink and never lets you get the best out of yourself. Mostly it stops you from enjoying life and makes you take everything you see around you for granted.

Taking the time to set aside 20 minutes a day just to turn your brain off can do wonders for your self-esteem, because it puts you into a better emotional state. The state we are in determines how good we feel about ourselves in the moment, so if you are excited, you would act different compared to if you were depressed. The happier I feel throughout the day has changed because I made a real decision on what I wanted and applied it, just like with anything in life.

You get rewarded by disciplining yourself and it makes you wake up five years down the track with no regret. Discipline weighs ounces regret weighs tonnes. So, I always give people the 2week test which means you are going to set a time every morning that you force yourself to meditate and by giving yourself this discipline it will make your feel alive because you're making progress.

Whenever a human being feels like they are making progress on something, they feel the most alive and happy. I will give you a mediation exercise to do so you can apply it straight away and get results.

Mediation Exercise
1. Get comfortable and pay attention to your breathing and just keep your focus on you breathing in and out.

2. It's okay to wonder off but it's all about catching yourself wondering and bringing yourself back to centre.

3. You can repeat a mantra over and over again in your head to keep your focus just on one thing at a time.

4. Set an alarm for 15minutes and even if you want to stop keeping pushing and something will shift.

Chapter 11. The Biggest Mistakes Of Anger Management

Though you have extensive knowledge about anger management now, it does not mean that you will be free and clear from the struggles that this recovery process will bring on. There will be moments that are harder to deal with than all the other things that you have experienced in your life as an angry person. It is unfortunate that we can't simply take a pill or get surgery to remove the anger from our system. It will always play a role in who we are. It matters when moving forward that we put a focus on accepting anger as it is and preparing for it instead of trying to pretend that we are out of the woods with this challenging emotion.

It is important to recognize how anger can present itself in other aspects of your life. Even though it might feel like you are free and clear from this somewhat dangerous emotion, you won't always be able to escape its grip. Always look at the challenging, annoying, agitating, and frustrating situations to see if your emotional reaction has played any part in how you feel. After that, discover what emotion is seemingly dormant underneath this anger to drive it to a place that causes so many issues and do not allow yourself to make any of these mistakes again.

Always break cycles when you see them. That is how you will be able to truly work towards a better life.

Substance Abuse

When we feel like something is missing, we can sometimes decide to find another activity to fill that hole. This can be done with any sort of substance that fills us with good emotions, endorphins, and dopamine, which relieves the underlying issues that drive anger to the surface. If you are socially anxious, to the point that you get a little sassy with others, then you may drink to try to keep your emotions at bay. You tend to eat more often as well because you know you will be less likely to snap at someone if you have a full belly.

Your mind can easily become addicted to anything that will make it feel better. This is why we might get addicted to drugs, food, alcohol, sex, and so on. These things make us feel good. Our brain remembers that good feeling and tells us later when we're not feeling so great that we should do use or consume that thing that we have liked earlier. This is our brains' attempt at trying to self-medicate.

Those with anger management issues can become very addicted to such substances. Some people might have even said to you at one point in your life, "You are nicer when you are drunk." This can be because we are alleviating stress and anxiety that causes anger. This is only momentarily, however; it is like putting a band-aid on an infected wound. We must treat the core problem to ensure that we do not have to live with it again.

Alcohol, sex, and other potentially addictive substances can be fun to have in small doses. They might help you to loosen up and have a good time as well. The way to know if you are having a problem is if you are treating it like a medicine. If you come home from work, pissed off, and you want to crack a beer, this is okay. This habit is not acceptable to do every night, however. The enjoyment of these potentially addictive substances should be for celebration, not medication.

Sleep and Diet

Make sure that you are properly taking care of yourself by getting the right amount of sleep and eating things that are good for you. You might be surprised at how poor nutrition is not just affecting your body but your mental health as well.

Too much sleep can lead to depressive moods, more lethargy, and an overall sense that you haven't quite accomplished something in a day. Any of these can be triggering for your anger, so ensure that you are taking the proper steps to find the right balance of sleep.

Not enough will make you feel angry and groggy. If we're consistently anxious, then we might also discover that it is hard to sleep. If you are having trouble falling asleep, try a warm tea without caffeine before bed. Read as well or even listen to a meditation to keep you in a deeper sleep.

Foods to Avoid

There are some foods that might even increase your anger. Thus, you should practice an elimination diet if you believe that something you are eating can heighten this emotion. This technique will involve taking away one food at a time for a controlled period so that you can see if that causes any food-related symptoms. Someone who's trying to find the foods that make them sick may start with removing cheese, yogurt, then other dairy products. If that doesn't work, maybe they can get rid of meat, certain veggies, and even gluten. This should all be done over weeks so that each food choice gets its own time. This way, you can figure out which one causes nutritional imbalances.

The food that you eat is not necessarily indicative of your anger issues, but it is worth exploring for people with chronic anger. Red and hot foods have been known to inflate some feelings of anger in the past. The spices can keep our bodies working harder, and they will cause hormonal imbalance, which allows us to snap immediately. Try removing spicy foods for a week to see if that helps decrease your hot temper.

If you are not eating healthy foods and only allowing processed junk into your diet, this can be damaging as well. Processed foods have additives that can cause inflammation. When you get a cut, have you noticed how the skin around the cut gets red and puffy? The wound gets inflamed because your body is fighting off outside sources, considering you are eating additives that are found in highly processed food that your body doesn't know how to react to. Only, you do not see that this inflammation can sometimes even occur in your brain. This can lead to heightened feelings of stress and anxiety and inhibit your brain from releasing the proper amounts of dopamine and serotonin. Therefore, you should ensure that you are reducing inflammation by incorporating antioxidant-rich foods in your diet, such as spinach, raspberries, and pomegranates.

You might find that journaling is the best way to figure out what foods you should eat or avoid. You can keep track of what you consume along with the symptoms that you feel when eating a food.

Cutting out some of these foods out does not mean that you can never eat them again. You can combat them with cooling foods, such as tea or even aloe. Simply identify the source of anger in your diet and decide from there if it is something that needs removed or simply treated (Steber, 2019).

Bottling Up Anger

Some people will think that if you bottled up, repress, and keep anger to yourself, it will make you angrier in the end. You might eventually snap and have an explosive outburst on a person who has triggered the emotions. However, it is not necessarily true that this situation can heighten your anger.

We can draw the conclusion that perhaps it simply attaches that aggressive response in your brain to something that is valid. When you lose a card game and you end up punching a wall, it does not make you madder per se. Instead, the aggressive act turns out to the solution for the anger that you feel. Next time you feel angry, your brain will remember that this is the appropriate response. It doesn't make you feel any better, though; it merely validates the idea that you should use aggression to solve your anger.

Though you are not taking aggression out on another person, you are still acting aggressively. You might get to a point where normal amount of aggression do not satisfy you anymore. Punching walls may have helped at first, but now you are looking for a bigger reaction, so you might hit a friend next time you feel angry. Though it feels good, remember that this is just the adrenaline being released. Find other ways to alleviate this desire through acts that aren't aggressive.

We are not saying that anger will merely go away or dissolve into nothingness. We still have issues when we decide to bottle up our emotions. The process involves trying to make your anger simply go away. The root needs to be dug out and disposed of; otherwise, the issues will keep on coming back. You can continue to bury the root, too, if you like, but it will always grow back and sprout from the dirt that you have used to cover it.

There might be some days when it feels particularly hard to express yourself, and you might assume that you simply need to get your anger out. The truth is that it will not help at all; it can make you feel even worse. Find a productive way to express this anger, such as going for a run or solving a puzzle. Your brain will then start to associate anger with doing something relaxing. This helps train your perspective, so when you find yourself angry later, your brain will naturally try to soothe itself instead of focusing on aggression (Markman, 2019).

- Knowing the mistakes of others while going through anger management recovery can ensure that you are not making your own.
- Substance abuse is your mind's attempt at fixing the problems that exist within your brain. This is just a temporary solution and not a long-term fix that will genuinely benefit you.
- The foods you eat and the amount of sleep that you get can directly affect how angry you might feel on any given day.

- Bottling up your anger and taking it out on others is never healthy. Anger needs to be confronted so that you can work it out, not hope that it merely goes away.

Chapter 12. Solid Tips For Boosting Emotional Self-Awareness

The first step towards developing greater emotional intelligence is boosting self-awareness, or your understanding of your own feelings and emotions. You can regulate your emotions for an optimally positive outcome only if you are able to identify these emotions. Labeling emotions and determining your actions based on these emotions is critical to the process of developing emotional intelligence. When you are more aware of your feelings and emotions, recognizing other people's emotions becomes simpler.

Here are solid, proven tips for boosting self-awareness to get you started on the path of emotional intelligence:

Label your emotions

Label and categorize your emotions. I know this makes your feelings sound like they belong to a library. However, labeling, or giving names to your emotions, makes it easier to identify and act upon them. When you feel an emotion surging through you, attempt to identify it quickly. Is it fear, insecurity, jealousy, anger, elation, depression, surprise, or a combination of these emotions?

Identify the triggers that cause these emotions. For instance, a specific person may evoke jealousy in you because you feel they are more successful than you.

What makes you feel certain emotions? What are the triggers that anger or hurt you? What makes you happy and sad? What is the source of positive and destructive emotions in you? Labeling your feelings and recognizing the stimuli for various emotions will increase your emotional self-awareness.

Grab a pen and paper to list your emotions when you experience a compelling feeling. Mention the precise emotion or feeling that you are experiencing. Accompany this emotional label with the trigger that caused it. What is it that made you feel the way you do? When you recognize an emotion, it is easier to manage it.

For instance, let us assume you feel a deep sense of loathing for a person without any specific reason. You dislike them and can't stand them, but funnily, can't tell why you dislike them. Upon closer examination of your feelings, you realize you dislike them because you are envious of them. You may believe they are always having a wonderful life, while things never go your way. By nailing this emotion as jealousy, you can regulate your potentially negative emotions.

Once you recognize the emotion as irrational jealousy, you will view it in a more logical and understanding manner. You'll begin to think along the lines that it isn't really someone's fault that they lead an amazing life. In fact, they should be applauded for working hard towards their goals. You'll realize that no one has a perfect life. Everyone goes through shares of trials and tribulation to attain success, which isn't necessarily visible to the outside world. Sometimes, it is only how we perceive things and not the reality. Thus, once you are more mindful of your emotions, you can work with them more positively.

Be an expert on yourself

What is the one thing you should do to bring about changes in your thoughts, actions, and behavior? The answer is: awareness about these thoughts and subsequent actions! To make changes, you ought to know what you have to improve upon.

Knowing yourself inside out is the key to being more emotionally aware and savvy. Did you know athletes are trained to identify and overcome feelings before an important upcoming game? This is based on the premise that if you can successfully identify and control your emotions, it doesn't impact your productivity.

Go back and think about all the recent instances where you let emotions get the better of you and affect your productivity. Haven't you let trivial matters impact your performance?

By being aware of your strengths and weaknesses, it is easier to confidently accomplish your objectives. There is a lesser scope for frustration, low productivity, and disappointment. Self-confidence increases your assertiveness while you express your thoughts and opinions, which is important for developing social skills.

Once you gain greater awareness, you will rarely be ruled by emotions. You have a clear edge if you are able to regulate your emotions. An emotionally aware person stops being a victim of his emotions and uses these emotions in a positive way to reach a desired outcome.

Spend time recognizing areas of development to strengthen them

- List all your strengths and weaknesses.
- Take a formal, psychological personality assessment test that helps you discover your own skills, abilities, limitations, and values.
- Obtain objective feedback from people you trust.

One way that works wonders for increasing your self-awareness is journaling. Write in a flowing stream of consciousness about the thoughts you are feeling and experiencing as they are occurring. What are the emotions you are experiencing? What are the physiological reactions to your feelings? Are you experiencing a faster heartbeat, sweaty palms, increased pulse, etc. as a physical reaction to your emotions?

Emotions aren't always straightforward. In fact, they are complex and multi-layered. For example, you may have a heated argument with your partner and feel angry, hurt, upset, and vengeful all at the same time. Write emotions exactly as you are experiencing them, even if two emotions appear to contradict each other. For instance, if you've got a scholarship to study overseas, you may be elated at the opportunity. However, the thought of leaving behind your partner may cause a twinge of sadness, too. You are acknowledging and validating your emotions by writing them.

Do a frequent check-in

Do a frequent check-in with your emotions much like how you have a waiter checking in with you frequently to know if you need anything. You do a mental check-in of your emotions periodically to understand how you are feeling at different times during the day. It is a sort of, "Hello, mind, how are you feeling? What can be done to make you feel better?"

Examine the origin of these specific feelings. Are you feeling low and deflated because your boss said something to you in the morning? Are you feeling angry and hurt because you fought with your partner? Are you experiencing certain physiological symptoms as a result of these emotions or feelings? Are these emotions impacting your body language, posture, gestures, and expressions? Are these emotions evident or visible to others? Are you more transparent when it comes to expressing your emotions? Are your decisions primarily determined by emotions?

If you want to be a more emotionally balanced person, reconnect with your primary emotions, recognize them, accept the emotions, and use them for making better decisions.

Use third person

Research in the field of labeling our emotions has indicated that when we distance ourselves from our emotions, or view them more objectively, we gain higher self-awareness. Next time you feel the urge to say, "I am disappointed," try to say, "Jack is disappointed."

If that seems too preposterous, try saying, "I am presently experiencing sadness," or, "One of my feelings at the moment is sadness."

These are techniques through which you are distancing yourself from overpowering emotions to stay naturally composed. You are basically treating your emotions as just another piece of information rather than being overwhelmed by them.

Each time you find yourself experiencing an urge to react to a situation, take a moment to name it. Then use it in the third person to distance yourself from intense emotions.

Emotions don't always need to be fixed

You don't always have to identify emotions with the intention of fixing them. Self-awareness is not about fixing emotions. It is about recognizing these emotions and letting them pass rather than allowing them to get the better of you. Society has conditioned us to think that certain emotions are bad. We mistakenly believe that experiencing these emotions makes us a bad person.

Far from it, emotions aren't good or bad. They are just that, emotions. There's no need to push away the seemingly bad emotions. Acknowledge that you are experiencing an emotion by saying something like, "I am experiencing jealousy." Practice deep breathing for a while until the emotion passes. Rather than pushing the emotion away and, in the process, increasing its intensity to come back even stronger, gently acknowledge it and let it be until it passes.

It takes around six seconds for the body to absorb chemicals that can alter your emotions. Give your body that much time.

We often share a hostile relationship with our emotions. They are believed to be something that is negative and should be fought or suppressed. However, emotions are information that helps us function in our daily lives. Overcome the mindset that emotions are good or bad, and instead focus on using them to empower you. Rather than letting emotions take control of you, use emotional information to work with them.

Emotions are neural hormones that are released as a direct response to our perceptions regarding the world. They direct us towards a specific action. All emotions have a distinct message and objective, which means there's no such thing as a good or bad emotion.

For example, fear helps us focus on an impending danger and take the necessary action to defend ourselves. Similarly, sadness makes us experience a sense of loss and facilitates a better understanding of what we truly care about.

If you move away from your best friend and become sad, this mean you truly care about them so much that you experienced sadness. This is valuable information. Hence, sadness is not a bad emotion. It can be used to identify what you care about.

If you use emotions as information for recognizing feelings, they can be channeled positively. The number one rule for developing higher emotional intelligence is to stop judging and curbing your emotions.

Train yourself to identify emotions based on physiological reactions

Our emotions often have physical manifestations. For example, you may feel anxious before a job interview or an important presentation. You experience the sensation of having 'butterflies in your stomach' before addressing an audience on the stage.

Don't you find your heart pounding with excitement when you are about to go on a date with someone you've fancied for long? Nervousness leaves us with sweaty palms and stiff muscles.

While these are only some of the physiological reactions we experience with our emotions, research has proven that a variety of emotions are strongly associated with stimulating certain parts of the body.

Regular patterns of physical sensations are linked with each of the six fundamental emotions, including fear, happiness, anger, sadness, disgust, and surprise. Human emotions discreetly overlap physiological sensations. For example, lower limb sensations are associated with sadness. Similarly, increased upper limb sensations are connected with anger. A strong feeling of disgust generates sensations within the throat and digestive system. Fear and surprise generate sensations in the chest.

Identify recurring patterns

This can be one of the most effective parts of knowing yourself. Neuroscience will help you understand the process more effectively. Our brains have an inherent tendency to follow established neural paths rather than creating new ones. This doesn't necessarily mean that the established patterns are serving us positively or that they can't be altered.

For instance, when a person becomes angry, he or she may bottle up their emotion rather than express it. This has become an emotional pattern with the person and is deeply embedded in the mind. However, awareness of this pattern can help the person chart another course of action, where the person practices responding instead of simply reacting to the emotion. However, the first step to charting a new pattern is identifying a pattern.

Recognize the build-up of emotions before something suddenly triggers you. These triggers have a predictable pattern. If you are already frustrated, you are more likely to see a situation in a more negative light. Similarly, if you are overcome by fear, you are more likely to interpret a stimulus as a threat. It is therefore important to be aware of these biases and how they can impact our emotions by creating a predictable pattern. The more efficient you become in recognizing your biases, the lower your chances of misinterpreting a stimulus.

Work with what you know about emotions

Emotions are important pieces of data that help you gauge things from a clearer and objective perspective. Don't suppress, ignore, fight, or feel overwhelmed by your emotions. Instead, you should build a valuable library of experiences with them. The purpose of emotional awareness is to concentrate our attention on these emotions and use them positively to create the desired outcome.

Treat your emotions as data that relies on your view of the world, or as a guide on how to act. When you open yourself to this data, you enjoy access to a huge resource of emotions that can be utilized to drive your actions in the right direction. You will know exactly how to reach wherever it is that you want to go if you have a clear emotional route. Therefore, you should acknowledge and recognize your emotions as data, and work with them instead of trying to beat them.

Begin by carefully noticing how you feel at the moment. Observe emotions without judging them or attempting to fix them. Learn to simply notice your emotions.

Be receptive to feedback and constructive criticism

One of the best ways to develop greater awareness of your emotions is to be more open to feedback and criticism from others. For instance, a friend may tell you that each time they talk about their accomplishments they sense your pangs of envy or dislike towards them. This may help you tune into your emotions and emotional triggers more effectively.

Emotionally intelligent folks are open to receiving feedback, and they always consider the other person's point of view. You may not necessarily agree with them but listening to other people's criticism and feedback helps you work on your blind spots. This can help you recognize your thoughts, triggers, and behavioral patterns.

I know a person who, in a bid to increase his self-awareness and emotional quotient, actively goes around asking people for feedback about his words, feelings (as they understand it), and actions. It acts as an emotion meter, which helps him gain greater awareness of his emotions and regulate them more efficiently.

Chapter 13. Tips For Anger Management

Self-Help Tips for Anger Management

You've realized your problem, you've decided that you are going to solve it no matter what, and you've taken the first step. The most essential thing you need to know at the beginning of this rigorous process is that, while it is not going to be easy, you need to take one step at a time. Your anger issues will not be solved overnight, and you will not be able to get rid of the frustration following the tips one time. It is a trial-and-error process, and you are going to have to figure out what works best for you. However, at the end of the line is a calm, composed, and emotionally stable person that you've always wanted to be and the journey really isn't that long!

The first step in the journey is to mentally acknowledge your anger. Running away from it, avoiding how you feel, and simply blaming your frustration on an unrelated source will do you no good. Anger is not necessarily negative and needs to be acknowledged before it can be dealt with. However, acknowledging the presence of anger must never be confused with the inappropriate expression of it. Even after you accept the fact that it is there, there must be a systematic managed way for you to express it in.

Immediate Calming Techniques

In order to eradicate feelings of anger and hostility, you essentially need to look into the causes of it and deal with them directly. However, this is a long-term process that improves gradually. Meanwhile, you need to acquaint yourself with techniques that you can use to immediately calm yourself when you feel angry. Depending on your method of expression, you can decide what works best for you and work towards stabilizing your mood and your behavior in that very moment. Speculation comes later.

For most people, extreme anger is characterized by the need to shout, hit something, or just by feeling physically restless and frustrated. For this, regardless of the reason, there are a number of relaxing techniques that you can use.

Deep breathing – Give yourself some alone time immediately and practice deep breathing. Make yourself aware of your body and focus on a single, slow breath, picturing it coming up as you release it. Repeat this a few times until you feel more relaxed.

Soothing imagery – Everyone has their own idea of a place where they would feel calm and relaxed. Whether from memory or from imagination, think of a place, person, or belonging that will help you calm down. The idea of this is to picture something that you cannot emotionally associate with anger or hostility.

Motivating words – Tell yourself to repeatedly 'relax' or 'calm down'. Simply repeating the words in your head sometimes can provide the distraction and the conviction needed.

Relax your body – Every time you feel the tension building up in your body, especially if you are used to physical aggression, sit down and relax all the muscles in your body. Calming down your body physically can calm your mind and distract it from the stressful situation.

Healthy release – Unlike what you have commonly heard, using forms of venting that depict aggression themselves is not healthy. No, you should not punch a bag to let your frustration out. Instead, if you are still feeling cranky about that fight you had at work, go running. Running, along with other exercises, releases oxytocin, which decreases stress levels in the body.

Staying Calm During An Argument

One of the most difficult parts of being angry is having a conversation while you are going through this complex mix of feelings. You may be used to shouting in an argument or saying things that you do not completely mean and know you will regret later but cannot seem to stop yourself from doing it. If this is the case, you can follow a number of strategies to make sure that a small argument does not turn into something entirely different.

Remember the purpose – Keep reminding yourself mentally that the purpose of your conversation is to solve the problem, not to aggravate it. Therefore, be careful that what you say is simple and straightforward, and the aim of it is to get your message across only, not to ridicule, hurt, or control the recipient.

Don't stray from the topic – We have all had those times when we were having an argument with a significant other over a tiny issue, which then ended up being something completely different, and both the parties were exhausted and hurt. Remind yourself of the problem that you are talking about, and do not pick on other problems, remember past issues and restate them, or directly attack someone's respect.

Breaking Down Emotions to Find Solutions

If you have been feeling cranky for a while and are not feeling better despite there being no apparent issue or, perhaps, a minor issue that should not incite such a reaction, give yourself some time to think. Ideally, this should be after your initial anger has faded away and you are left with the lingering feeling of annoyance and irritability. Think about what might be bothering you and break the issue down. Ideally, you can write this down to get a clearer understanding of what you are looking at.

Once you have come up with the specific issue that is bothering you, your aim should be to counter it with logic. Remember: logic trumps anger! With the latter mostly being irrational, finding your way to a logical explanation might just be the solution you need. If you have been feeling cranky for days after you had a fight with your spouse over not spending enough time together, sit down and begin writing the reasons this could be. Ask yourself if the two of you want to spend time together. If the answer to that is yes, list the reasons that cause you to not have enough time. If you both have different working hours, for example, that shows the reason is entirely legitimate and being angry with yourself or your spouse is irrational.

Similarly, if you realize that the reason for your anger is low self-esteem and your behavior is usually a defense mechanism every time someone criticizes you, use logic to prove your own negative thoughts wrong. If someone criticized you at work, list down all the times that someone appreciated you, and then think about why they might have criticized you this time. Logical reasoning, along with seeing everything in a positive light, is what will eventually make you see that your reasons for being aggressive might not even be justified.

Once you reach logical reasons for a situation, you can then look for similar solutions. Working out a problem this way and not through continuous anger and negative feelings will give you a sense of reasoning with yourself, which will, after a while, become a healthy habit. Also, noting down the reasons every time you feel angry will allow you to observe a pattern and identify the main triggers for your anger.

Cognitive Restructuring

Cognitive processes are the thoughts that you go through in any given situation. In order to avoid overthinking in stressful situations and to trigger rage, one of the key solutions is to restructure the way you think. While this is not an immediate solution, it is something that you need to practice regularly over time to get the best results. Over the course of a few months or years, you can be a calmer person not only outwardly but also at a mental level.

Accept and love yourself – No matter how impossible it seems to stop the flow of thoughts that fills you when you feel frustrated, you need to know that you are the owner of your mind, and you *can* control it. For one, you need to take away all the negative feelings associated with anger. For example, instead of telling yourself "I am an extremely aggressive person with a severe problem, and I cannot control myself at all," think about the problem in a more positive light. Tell yourself, "I have a problem, but I have the potential to solve it, and knowing this is the first step to my recovery."

Look at things in a positive light – The best way to go on about restructuring your cognitive processes is to look at minor words and things that make you think in an extreme manner. For example, try to remember what you think when you have a fight with your wife. Instead of thinking, "We always end up fighting; this is a horrible relationship," remind yourself of the times that you do not fight. When one is angry, it becomes extremely difficult to see the good side of things, and that is exactly what you need to learn.

Filter your vocabulary – Remember that the way you think and the words that you use vocally or in your mind are the ones that aggravate the way you feel. Start practicing eliminating extreme words from your vocabulary. For example, don't use words like "never" and "always." Don't think, "My boss always criticizes me" or "My wife never understands how I feel." Instead, choose calmer words that depict an average intensity. The best way to do this is to begin by watching what you say and trying to keep a check on your vocabulary. Gradually, this will automatically incorporate into the way you think, as well.

Meditation

When your aggression is something that has control over your entire life, you cannot expect it to go away simply by using relaxing techniques at the moments of rage. If you have severe aggression problems, you will gradually need to bring small changes in your overall lifestyle, regardless of the times when you feel angry. One of these positive and healthy changes can be meditation. It has been known to instill a sense of calm in a person and can be a great way to connect with yourself.

Often, you feel frustrated simply because you are a little too caught up in daily life activities to spend time trying to rejuvenate your mind. Instead, you keep going through a rigorous routine every day, straining your mental peace along the way. Taking some time out to meditate can be a great way to find your connection with the self-back, and to refresh the mental energy that you need to deal with everyday tasks. Naturally, if you go to work feeling calmer and happier with yourself, small things that other people do will not tick you off too much.

The way you meditate can be entirely your choice. Whether you want to resort to morning yoga or to simply find some time to talk to yourself in self-motivating, reinforcing language, what you need to focus on is releasing the negative energy and replacing it with calm.

Maintaining A Support System

Anger management is a difficult process that can drain you emotionally and is not something you can always do alone. Therefore, creating a support system around yourself is what might be the key factor in getting you through the process.

Tell someone about your plans – Whether a parent, a friend, or a spouse, there should be someone who knows about your problem and about the fact that you are struggling to solve it. Having someone to support your effort, to motivate you again when you fail, and to honestly judge whether or not you are getting better can be a great help.

Improve communication – Sometimes, the lack of a support system can be the very reason for the anger itself. Maybe you feel angry with your coworkers all the time because you have never bothered to listen to what they have to say and do not understand their viewpoint. Maybe you fight with your wife because, although you both want to be happier with each other, you refuse to budge from what you believe. Taking some time to talk to people with an open mind and understand their perspective might just eliminate the very reasons that make you feel frustrated. Just like yourself, everyone has an opinion of their own, and disagreements do not have to mean that someone is wrong.

Dedicate some time to those you love – Most psychologists believe that one of the major reasons of frustration and stress today is the lack of healthy communication. Working ten hours a day and then coming home tired barely leaves you any time to spend with your significant other. Tell yourself that you need time for those you love, and then stick to the plans you make. Take a day out every week with no particular work plans, and simply go with the flow. Go out with the people you love, take a refreshing walk, or simply stay in and talk and connect with each other. Sometimes, loving and feeling loved can be all the positive energy you need to drive our negative feelings like anger, stress, frustration, and hostility.

Recording Your Progress and Staying Persistent

Dealing with anger can also be very difficult because sometimes, you might feel like none of the techniques you are using are working. After having avoided anger for two days, an angry outburst on the third day might make you feel like you are not making any progress and are back to square one.

In order to avoid such feelings of failure, there are a number of methods you can use to stay positive.

Tell yourself that the process will take time – Anger is something that builds over the entire course of one's life. Naturally, you cannot expect it to away soon and you cannot expect to quit all of a sudden. Be prepared to spend a lot of time getting better, to try a number of methods to get over, and to fail sometimes but to always get back up with a renewed spirit.

Record your progress – Make not only mental but written notes of how you feel now. Keep a journal where you record every time you felt angry, the thoughts you experienced during that time, and how long the feelings lasted. As you go on practicing anger management, keep recording instances of rage. Even if there is small decrease in these, you know that you are getting better.

Notice the problems – Sometimes, simply recording your progress may show you a pattern your rage seems to be following. Perhaps you always feel the angriest when you get home after a long day of work, in which case you can resort to relaxing activities when you get back or to lower your workload. Maybe you are frustrated the most when you get stuck in traffic, for which you can begin to take another route or change the time at which you travel. Making small changes in timings and finding alternatives for things that make you angry can sometimes make a bigger change in you than you think it will.

Appreciate yourself – Set milestones for yourself and be proud of yourself when you reach then. Tell yourself that the next time you have a fight with your wife, you will avoid saying hurtful things and will simply speak your mind about the problem at hand. When you manage to do this, appreciate yourself and set a higher milestone for next time. Another great way to feel motivated is to talk to a friend about your anger management process and tell them about the progress you are making. A little appreciation can really go a long way to keep you motivated!

Tips for Parents

A lot of parents seem to think that by sending an angry child to his room, it will help him calm down. Well, what else can be done? You might think that reasoning with an angry child is not a good idea. After all, it is not an ideal time to teach your young one when he is furious. You probably think that sending him to his room will calm him down and then you can talk to him about his anger. If you send him to his room, he will calm down. He will calm down eventually, even if not immediately. However, it will also give him a wrong message, and he will come to the following conclusions.

- That no one will listen to him when he is upset.
- Anger is a terrible emotion that will always lead to some form of punishment.
- No one will help solve the problem that he seems to be experiencing.
- That he must not express his anger if he wants to avoid being sent to his room.
- When angry, he might think the best way to go about it ignores any powerful emotions he feels.

Well, none of these conclusions are good, and they all encourage the formation of negative associations with anger. Therefore, it is not a surprise that a lot of people have anger issues even in their adulthood. The way your child learns to deal with his anger will have a major effect on his life in the future. Instead of doing this, as a parent, it is your responsibility to help your child positively deal with anger. Most parents have trouble understanding how they can teach their children to deal with anger positively. Simply put, the responsible way to manage one's anger starts with understanding and acknowledging the emotion without lashing out at others. You can always express your anger without harming others, and you must teach your kids about the same.

When you take a moment and notice the underlying feelings of one's anger, you might notice other emotions like fear, hurt, or even sadness. Once you allow yourself to experience these underlying emotions, anger will fade away. Most of us tend to use anger as a defensive mechanism. A critical lesson a child must learn is to tolerate any problems in daily life without getting angry. Those who learn this skill in their childhood tend to have the necessary emotional intelligence to keep going in life and can keep their emotions in check in their adult life too.

In this section, you will learn about a couple of things that you must do when your child gets angry.

Keep Calm

Usually, parents tend to either yell or challenge their child in case of an angry outburst. When you do this, you will merely increase the feeling of helplessness and stress on the child being out of control. The best thing to do while dealing with an angry outburst is to keep your calm. For instance, if you get into an accident and the other driver jumps out of the car and starts yelling at you, if you remain calm, it is quite likely that the other driver will calm down too. However, if you respond aggressively, it is quite likely that the situation will become tenser than it already was. So, instead of challenging your child when he seems to be angry or upset, you must wait patiently until he is calm enough to talk.

Listen to Your Child

A lot of parents tend to ignore the reasons that make their child angry. Do you like it when someone ignores you? Do you like it when you feel like no one is listening to you or that no one is acknowledging what you are saying? I am certain that you don't like any of these things. Well, even your child doesn't like it. If you want to teach your child to manage his anger, you must first acknowledge that your child is angry. Usually, a situation escalates when you ignore your child's anger. Instead of ignoring your child, help him feel like he is being understood and your child will stay calmer even if he doesn't get his way.

Talk to Him

Once your child is calm, you can start talking to him about his anger. Don't try to reason with him when he is upset. Instead, wait for him to regain his composure. Before you start talking to him about anger management, keep reassuring him that he is loved and safe.

The way you deal with your child when he is having an angry outburst will dictate the way he handles his anger. If he feels like he will be punished whenever he lashes out, he will start forming negative associations with anger. You must understand that anger is a basic and powerful emotion. Only when your child understands this will he be able to manage it effectively.

Never Get Physical

At times, parents tend to lose control. When this happens, they can get physical with their kids. For instance, a father might shove his son if he bad mouthed his mother. The fight will undoubtedly escalate, and there will be no end to it. If you want a way out, then you must ensure that you'll never get physical with your child, regardless of how much he pushes you. If you give in and react to the child aggression, it will only show the child that he has control over you, and you have no control over him. As a parent, this is something that you must try to avoid at all costs. If there comes a situation where you did get physical with your child, then ensure that you do apologize for it. Make sure that your apology is as genuine as you possibly can muster.

Empathy

Try to view the situation from your child's perspective. If you are compassionate toward your child, the easier it will be for your child to express himself. A little compassion can help your child address any underlying reasons that made him angry instead of the superficial anger that you can see. Even saying something as simple as, "Oh honey! I didn't mean for you to feel like you aren't understood. I know it must be so hard for you right now, and I am sorry for it." I am not saying that you must agree with your child's perspective. You neither have to agree nor disagree with him. You merely need to try and acknowledge his truth at present. Once he feels acknowledged and heard, his truth will also change.

Don't Take it Personally

Parents usually feel hurt when their kids yell at them. However, your child doesn't hate you, and the things they say when they are hurt aren't necessarily true. You must try to prevent any personal attacks from hurting you. Your child is lashing out because he probably feels scared, anxious, and powerless and is, therefore, lashing out at you. The rudeness might hurt, but at the moment, you must try to understand the cause of that rudeness instead of reacting to it. Ask your child why he is angry and reassures him that you are listening to all that he has to say. Your child is not trying to behave badly or win something. He is merely showing how upset he is in whatever way he can. Once he realizes that he doesn't need to lash out or throw a tantrum to get your attention or feel heard, he will be able to express himself freely. No one likes to feel vulnerable, and this stands true for kids too. So, once he knows that he can freely express himself, he will stop resorting to anger to do the same.

Establish Certain Limits

You must set certain limits to ensure that everyone stays safe while making your child feel like he is being acknowledged. You can tell your child that he can express his anger as long as he doesn't cause any physical harm to himself or those around them. For instance, you can tell him to stomp to display his anger, but he cannot hit anyone or himself, regardless of how angry he feels.

Reassure Your Child

If your child is having a complete meltdown, then the first thing you must do is reassure him that he is safe and show him some empathy. You can reason with him or teach him something later, but for now, ensure that he knows that he is in a safe place. When your child's fight or flight response kicks in, it is highly unlikely that he will want to listen to anything you say. Not just that, it is also quite likely that he will not understand what you are saying. Instead, show your child some empathy and offer some reassurance.

Immaturity of The Child

Please keep in mind that tantrums are the only way an immature brain knows to blow off steam. The frontal cortex in a child isn't fully developed yet. The best way to help in the development of the neural pathways in the frontal cortex is by offering the child some empathy when he is mad. Remember that your child doesn't know how to express anger in any other way and doesn't know how to manage his anger yet. Allow your child to express himself and reassure that you are with him even when he is angry. Once he is calm, he will be in a better position to listen to and understand what you are saying.

A Safe Environment

If your child feels like he can express his anger and if you are compassionate while he does this, it will help calm him. So, you must try to reassure your child that you will be there with him and wait for his anger to melt away. If the child knows that he is in a safe and loving space, it is easier for him to express what he is feeling or experiencing. If he has the confidence that he will be loved even when feeling vulnerable, it will prevent him from resorting to anger as a defense mechanism.

Don't Try to Reason

A lot of parents seem to think that reasoning with a kid when he is angry is a good idea. After all, adults use logic and reasoning to defuse an angry situation. However, you cannot reason with an angry kid because they don't have the same mental capacity as adults to understand the logic you're putting forth. So, when you are dealing with an upset child, forget about using logic for a while, especially when he is in the middle of an angry outburst. If you wish to talk to your child, then do so only after he has calmed down. If your child is having an angry outburst, then wait for him to finish. Don't stop him in the middle of it, as it will only make you more upset.

Observe Your Reactions

It is quintessential that you observe your reactions, mental as well as physical ones. When you're in the presence of someone having an angry outburst, your heart weight will be elevated. It is because of the adrenaline pumping through your veins. Even though it might be slightly tricky, the best thing that you can do is stay calm. Remember, the way you react in such a situation will affect the way your child behaves. If you stay calm and show them that you can deal with anger, the child will feel more secure and confident. However, if you challenge your child and engage in any form of power struggles, all it will do is add fuel to the fire. Also, by observing your reactions, you can help your child pay attention to his behavior since he doesn't have to worry about your reactions. When you don't keep your calm or react unfavorably, then all it does is egg your child to keep going.

Freeze Up

At times parents tend to either shout or freeze up while dealing with angry kids. The parents tend to feel so emotionally overwhelmed that they tend to become paralyzed while dealing with the child. If this happens to you, or if this has happened during the past, then you might notice that your child will get mad at you on purpose to engage such behavior. Your child is technically baiting you or throwing a fit because he knows that you will give in eventually. Please don't take this bait. At the same time, you must not get angry. At times, parents also tend to try and negotiate with a child while he is in the midst of throwing a temper tantrum. Often, parents tend to have a rather hard time understanding and managing their own emotions, so they don't know how to deal with an angry child. However, if you do give in or negotiate, then you're teaching your child that it is okay to act out. If your child comes to believe that there are no consequences to acting out, then he will do so more frequently.

It is okay not to negotiate. It does not make you passive. When you refuse to negotiate, you are making a conscious decision to end the argument.

Consequences Matter

You must understand that it is okay to set consequences for bad behavior but not for the younger. If your child starts throwing an anger tantrum, starts shouting and has an outburst, then ensure that you give him a consequence which is based on his bad behavior and not only the emotion he's been expressing. For instance, if your child starts swearing at you while having an angry outburst, then give him a consequence later for cursing. However, please don't direct consequence based on the anger or the fact that he too would have a temper tantrum. If you start punishing him for his anger, then he will start forming negative associations with this emotion. Anger is as essential an emotion like happiness. So, it is quite crucial that he has a healthy relationship with all his emotions and by punishing any of them; you are merely creating a negative belief in his mind that getting angry is equivalent to getting punished. Tell your child that it is okay to be angry, as long as he knows how to manage his anger.

Conclusion

Instead of getting angry and affecting the environment around you, voice your concern with kindness, and she will go out of her way next time to ensure that your mail is sorted.

Adopt better skills for communication. When people get angry, they are likely to mutter the meanest things that come to their minds, however unkind. Before you react, however, take a minute to stop and breathe. Give careful thought to what you intend to say, and if you feel the need to step aside from an angry conversation to calm down, do so, and then get back to the conversation.

Simple breathing and relaxation techniques can effectively soothe angry feelings. Practice doing them in a normal situation, and it will be easier to apply them in the heat of the moment. Some of these techniques include:

Attentive breathing: When you are angry, you tend to have shallow quick breaths. Therefore, to counter this, practice deep controlled slow breathing, ensuring that they rise from your belly rather than your chest.

Relax your muscles progressively: Progressive muscle relaxation involves tensing and then relaxing your muscle group one at a time. For example, if you begin working on your head muscles, proceed to your neck muscles, going downward up until you reach the muscles in your toes.

Visualize what a relaxation experience would look like from your imagination. In the heat of an argument, visualize what the ideal situation would be, what it would look like without this conflict, and work towards achieving that.

Physical exercise done in the regular is a perfect decompression tool. It burns off the excess energy, releases the extra tension, and it lowers stress levels. When your body is all relaxed and all energy resources are being used appropriately, you are less likely to have anger outbursts.

Think about the things that cause you to lose it. If you know that driving during the rush-hour gets you angry, take the train or the bus, or at least plan to make your trip at a different time of the day. If you often go to bed arguing with your spouse, avoid bringing up contentious issues in the evening. If seeing your child's messy room gets you angry, shut the door, and you won't have to see the mess.

BOOK 3

Introduction

I bet you've been in a situation where you just get so angry that you can't do anything. Maybe it's your boss yelling at you, or your wife nagging, but no matter what the anger is about, whether it's justified or not, the truth is that anger does not solve anything. The time for talk is over; now it's time to take action!

So how do we go about managing our anger? First of all, try and understand why it may be hard to control your emotions. Examine the situation more calmly and thoughtfully before reacting to the situation around you. This way, you can avoid being taken by surprise by your anger. Also, try to see the positive side of the situation (the good) and try not to dwell on negativity. Remember that it's impossible to just not feel angry about a specific event—it's something that happens in our lives every day.

Now for some tips and tricks for how to manage your anger:

Destroy emotional bridges right away: Going into an angry rant usually only leads to increased emotions, which might lead you down a useless path filled with regret and shame. Don't let anyone decide or tell you how you should feel about anything. Because of this realization, communication becomes much easier (your partner will feel safe talking things out with you).

Go into an angry rant usually only leads to increased emotions, which might lead you down a useless path filled with regret and shame. Don't let anyone decide or tell you how you should feel about anything. Because of this realization, communication becomes much easier (your partner will feel safe talking things out with you). Do your thinking outside of anger: Look at the situation from a third person perspective. You don't have to agree with what is happening, but rather try to understand what it all means. By taking a step outside of yourself, you can see the bigger picture.

Look at the situation from a third person perspective. You don't have to agree with what is happening, but rather try to understand what it all means. By taking a step outside of yourself, you can see the bigger picture. Put your anger on a shelf: This is one of the harder things to do, but with practice it gets easier. Take a few minutes to calm down and then analyze why you are angry. Then find out what will happen next and finally consider how the situation will be resolved (and then look for the positive aspect of that decision).

This is one of the harder things to do, but with practice it gets easier. Take a few minutes to calm down and then analyze why you are angry. Then find out what will happen next and finally consider how the situation will be resolved (and then look for the positive aspect of that decision). Accept your anger: Don't try to get rid of it or make it go away—instead, hold onto it for a bit and see what is really making you angry. You will feel better once you let go of the anger itself.

Don't try to get rid of it or make it go away—instead, hold onto it for a bit and see what is really making you angry. You will feel better once you let go of the anger itself. Accept your mate's anger: This one might be a hard pill to swallow (especially if your partner's temper blows up more often than yours) but remember that we all have different ways of dealing with our emotions. You need to accept that your significant other might not be good at dealing with anger, but it is up to you to guide her toward a solution.

This one might be a hard pill to swallow (especially if your partner's temper blows up more often than yours) but remember that we all have different ways of dealing with our emotions. You need to accept that your significant other might not be good at dealing with anger, but it is up to you to guide her toward a solution. Get it off your chest: Frustration and anger can build inside of you to the point where you feel like you're going to explode.

Frustration and anger can build inside of you to the point where you feel like you're going to explode. Make a plan: Now that you've gotten all of your negative feelings out in the open, it's time to find a solution. What would be the best next step? What can you do to help make sure that something like this doesn't happen again? You don't have to be stuck in the situation; instead, think about what you can do right now in order to move forward.

Now that you've gotten all of your negative feelings out in the open, it's time to find a solution. What would be the best next step? What can you do to help make sure that something like this doesn't happen again? You don't have to be stuck in the situation; instead, think about what you can do right now in order to move forward. Compose yourself: No matter what happens, try not to let your anger get the best of you.

No matter what happens, try not to let your anger get the best of you. Recognize the problem: No matter how angry you are, pay attention to what's going on. Watch your tone of voice, because it will affect how others respond to you. But do not let this anger make you do irrational things (like, say, calling your partner a name).

No matter how angry you are, pay attention to what's going on. Watch your tone of voice, because it will affect how others respond to you. But do not let this anger make you do irrational things (like, say, calling your partner a name). Make it work for you: Don't act out your anger or use it as an excuse for poor behavior. Instead, harness your anger to work for you. If you are in a position to do something that can actually change the situation for the better, consider that.

Anger can be a good thing if it is channeled properly, but it can also have an extremely detrimental effect on your life and on your love life if you let it get the best of you. The most important thing is to remember that everyone makes mistakes. Remember that this problem is between the two of you. No one else has to be affected by what happens, and if two people are unhappy enough to not be able to work through this problem, then they really need to work on their issues. Work on being a better lover; don't let your anger make that impossible for you.

Anger management is centered around self-control, and one of the most effective ways to improve it is through meditation. It's not easy to sit still when you're mad or aggressive, but there are a number of tools that can help you reduce your anger while increasing your mindfulness.

You'll have a better chance at managing your anger when you understand what causes it in the first place — and that's where this blog will be helpful!

You can manage anger. It's not easy to do everything that you want to do when you're angry. But effective anger management will give you more options than simply having a good explosion or holding it in until you blow up again.

There is evidence that meditation directly reduces anger in several studies. The average participant who meditates for 6 weeks experiences a 50 percent reduction in angry feelings compared to those who do not meditate (. However, research on meditation and anger tends to focus on Buddhist techniques such as mindfulness, which are difficult to pass down through traditional medical channels. As a result, many people have difficulty accessing the benefits of meditation even though there is strong evidence supporting its effectiveness.

One reason that anger management and mindfulness meditation in particular are not widely used is that it can be difficult to find a good teacher.

You should use the first session or two as an exploration period, during which you try different techniques and see what works best for you. If your first teacher is not a good fit, consider finding another one to work with. If that doesn't work out, try a few more until you find someone who is inspiring to work with.

Fortunately, there are several other ways to learn mindfulness techniques, including through books and self-help guides. These resources are far less effective than working directly with a teacher — but if they're all you have access to, they can still help you manage your anger.

Managing anger is a lot like learning to speak a new language. You can't learn it all at once; you have to start at the beginning with simple, repetitive exercises until you get more advanced as your skills improve. In the same way, the most effective anger management techniques tend to involve repeated practice and learning new things each time you try them.

You are unlikely to be able to change every negative habit that you have in one session, but you can certainly alter some of them. If you try for a week to think about your habits, you can change the anger management techniques that you use.

Don't chain yourself to one technique. There is a wide range of techniques that can help you manage your anger and get what you want out of life, so don't get stuck with just one method. Try things out in different ways and don't give up until you find something that works best for you.

As a father, you know the challenges your child presents and how challenging managing both your personal and professional lives can be. Many studies have shown that what happens at home can affect children's performance in school and in their everyday lives. Healthy parents are more productive workers. Fathers need to be happy and balanced so they can be the best caretaker for their families that they are capable of being.

Here's the thing, if a dad is not happy with his life, he will be unhappy for his children and likely as well for his spouse. This can lead to anger management, which in turn leads to outburst of emotions that effect everyone. It's better that we examine ourselves and our lives to ensure a more balanced life.

For many men identifying the cause of anger can be difficult because they are expected to not show emotion and are often told by other men not to worry about such things- "I'm okay!" or "I have my ways!". It's important as a caring father and husband that you acknowledge this as being something that needs your attention so that you can work on getting better for your family's sake.

Chapter 1. What is the Concept of Anger Management?

The term "anger management" often describes the process of learning how to manage anger and deal with it in a healthy way. It is also a process that is pursued in an effort to reduce negative feelings like anxiety, fear, and rage or as part of rehabilitation after committing criminal acts.

Anger management can be achieved by first recognizing the triggers for anger and then dealing with them one at a time by identifying the underlying emotion and its origins. Treatments may involve cognitive behavioral therapy (CBT) or acceptance & commitment therapy (ACT). A third treatment approach could include dialectical behavior therapy (DBT), which focuses on mindfulness. Stress inoculation training (SIT) can also be used to teach how to deal with stressful events, including anger. SIT is a structured program in which people learn how to cope with stress by practicing how they would like to react when they encounter the situations that trigger their stress.

Anger management is a term that denotes the process of regulating and moderating responses to anger-evoking stimuli. The goal of anger management is to improve one's emotional, social, and physical health.

Anger management is a good deal more than simply learning how to tolerate being provoked by another person. Instead, it is a way of mitigating the effects of aggression - thus keeping one from getting into a fight or other harmful altercation.

Anger Management Classes are often offered as part of an intervention strategy for individuals who have shown evidence of aggressive or violent behavior or are at risk for developing such behavior.

The goals are twofold:

According to the Association for Applied and Therapeutic Humor, laughter is expressed as a physiological reaction, "Laughter is good medicine; it lightens up our lives and helps us cope with illnesses such as arthritis, heart disease and depression. Laughter also may help to relieve pain, according to a study by the Loma Linda University School of Medicine. It can raise your level of endorphins and encephalins, natural chemicals in the body that diminish pain." The American Medical Association says, "to laugh is to exercise one of the most important of all the human organs—the heart."

However, laughter can be used as a way to vent anger. It has been found that when people laughed with other people, they enjoyed spending time with, it had a positive effect on their moods. It also made them feel closer to those people and more willing to work with them when given an opportunity later on."

There are many biological and psychological reasons for anger. Anger is a very powerful emotional state that can have a significant impact on our emotional and physical health. Like sadness and fear, anger is an emotion that can be controlled by the individual in order to improve their lives. Anger occurs when anxiety is out of control. It can be caused by a number of things, including frustration, pressure, performance pressures, lack of control, lack of perspective or understanding, poor communication skills or relationships with others.

Often times people do not realize when they are in an angry state until they feel it coming on and then they do not know what to do about it. They might feel confusion or panic. Getting caught up in the emotions of being angry can control us instead of us being able to control it. This is when anger builds up and is expressed in a more aggressive way. Anger can be a warning sign that we need to change something that is happening in our lives or behavior, or if we are not taking care of ourselves physically, mentally, or emotionally. When we see anger as a problem, it's important to look deeper at what may be causing this feeling and then find healthy ways to release it from our bodies without hurting others.

If you recognize yourself in difficult situations, it is important to become aware of your emotions and control how they influence your actions. By being aware of the above situations, you can learn how to stop or manage them before they cause problems.

In today's world, people are increasingly strapped for time and at times feel rushed or pressured to accomplish tasks within a certain period of time. This can sometimes lead to the feeling of anger, which is an emotion that may be expressed in a number of ways: physical aggression (such as hitting someone), verbal aggression (using profanity or shouting), or passive/aggressive behavior (sarcasm, stubbornness).

The most common physical expression of anger is through violent behavior. Anger can also lead to violence when people feel they must accomplish something urgently and are pushed to meet unrealistic deadlines. It is also important to realize that anger can be directed at people or situations, leading to harmful behavior.

Anger can also be expressed through resentment and frustration. Feeling angry for long periods of time and not being able to find a way out of this state of mind can cause people to feel hopeless and helpless. This is where they begin to dig their heels in and do something rash or destructive in an effort to express the anger, they are feeling inside themselves. Anger can also lead to us developing poor behaviors; we either lash out in self-defense or shut down as a result of the anger we are feeling around us.

Anger is often expressed by people who are depressed, particularly when they do not have a support system. The depressed person is often unable to find the way out of their anger and this can lead to feelings of hopelessness. Other people can also be angry when they don't know how to express their upset feelings, or because they are being hurt or mistreated by others.

Other things that cause anger include: the inability to handle pressure, feeling out of control, experiencing stress. We may also experience anger when we are stuck in traffic. Being late for an appointment on time is a situation that can cause a person to feel angry. We may get angry if we are unable to anticipate failures or setbacks in our lives and this leads us to feel helpless.

It is also important to remember that anger is a choice, and it's possible to choose not to be angry. If you get angry when you are trying to make a decision, follow your impulse and don't think about it. Don't think by what another person has done or will do. If you know for sure that the other person will do something wrong, then take control of the situation and stop the person from doing anything wrong.

Anger is different from depression. They are opposites, and if they both last for long periods of time, they can be very dangerous as a result.

Anger in the Body

When we feel anger emotions, the body becomes involved as well. Many people feel fatigued and irritable after discussing something that has caused them anger. It is important to realize that this happens to everyone, and it happens because of our lack of knowledge in dealing with other people's emotions. We don't want to be mad at people or situations, but we are not able to control our anger in these situations.

Most often when you get angry you will start itching and your skin will also turn red. These are caused by the adrenaline that starts to flow in the body. This can also lead to a feeling of nausea, and sometimes even vomiting. The adrenaline that is released by our bodies when we feel anger reaches other systems in the body, and they will either release their energy or store it. Usually, it is stored and then later when you are relaxed you will feel better.

If you constantly feel angry, you might be suffering from an adrenal gland disorder. Some people have an overproduction of this gland which leads them to be overly angry all the time. They suffer more than others when they get angry which means they are overreacting when they do get angry at something or someone that does not deserve it.

If you have a lower adrenal gland, the pain that you feel will not be as intense and your body will be able to accept it more easily.

If you are in a bad mood, most likely there is something that triggers it. The first thing I suggest is to take a look at the foods you eat. An excess of protein can lead to irritable bowel syndrome which is one of the main reasons why people are in a bad mood. Be careful of foods that contain too much salt and sodium. If sugar has been added to your diet, then this will also trigger an increase in blood sugar which can result in a bad mood.

If you don't get enough sleep, this will result in your body being tired and your mind will not be able to concentrate on the tasks at hand. This can also lead to depression which is yet another reason why people are in a bad mood.

There are several different conceptualizations of anger management, some of which will vary depending on the individual and their experience with anger. However, in general, the term is used to describe a process by which one engages in anger-supportive behaviors. These can include identifying triggers before they happen, practicing calming techniques before responding to triggering situations and exercises such as journaling or painting.

Anger management can also be seen as a way for people who have been victims of circumstances - such as abuse - to move beyond destructive thoughts or actions towards themselves or others. Some people who have suffered abuse in the past turn to anger management for help. There is a possibility that people can develop more serious mental health conditions because of inadequate care, such as depression or posttraumatic stress disorder. With proper therapy there is a positive outlook for someone who has been through traumatic events in their life and has developed issues with anger as a result.

Chapter 2. Who is Dad in the Family?

Dad is a pretty important person in the family, no matter what. But some people might not know or never think to ask who's Dad in their family?

It's often said that fathers play a more important role in the family than mothers. What is this role and what does it entail? This will explore some ways that dads can help raise their children to be happy, well-rounded adults.

The role of dad in the family is often difficult to define. Raising children is a collaborative process, which involves parents working together to ensure that their children are well taken care of. Dads play an important role in this equation, and the diversity of their contributions can be admirable.

A father's influence on his child is powerful because he not only teaches them how to act towards others, but he also channels his own experiences with family and society into conversations about right versus wrong. As a result, dad has the power to shape his child's world view.

Fathers are important for instilling in their daughters the importance of relationships with men. The male counterpart to a woman shapes how she views relationships. A man who is disrespectful towards his wife or children does not provide his daughter with good role modeling when it comes to her future relationship with men.

A father's influence on his son is just as powerful. Studies have found that a father's love for his child has a long-term effect on the son's health. This does not mean that the son will be healthy or successful because of the relationship; it simply means that he will feel loved by someone and, as such, will be more likely to go out of his way to please others.

Moreover, being loved by dad makes a child feel good about himself. When dad is around and shares quality time with the child, this can help curb emotional outbursts (such as crying) or aggressive behavior (such as hitting).

The qualities that make a good dad are patience and empathy. These qualities are especially important for challenges that don't necessarily involve discipline or discipline outside of the home. Fathers who work long hours, for example, can feel tired and frustrated when they return home to spend time with their family, but they still have an obligation to provide for them in even the toughest of situations.

It is often said that fathers have a better sense of humor and fun than mothers. A caring father is also important for the child's physical or mental well-being, as children who feel good about themselves tend to function better in school and have better social interactions with others.

Fathers who spend quality time with their children are more inclined to be involved in extracurricular activities, which can help them build relationships with friends and learn new skills that will help them in their future careers. Fathers who don't spend enough time with their children are less likely to feel comfortable asking for such things.

Dads also teach their sons the importance of maintaining a strong relationship with their own fathers, which can carry over into adulthood. This type of relationship can help sons maintain their own families later in life.

Fathers have the opportunity to make an impact on their children's future while they are still young and impressionable. It is never too early or too late to start teaching children about moral values or to start instilling good habits in them.

The following are some ways that fathers can learn to be better parents.

First, take the time to spend quality time with each of your children. This is especially important for children who feel neglected or played with more than others. This doesn't mean that the father has to spend more individual time with one child, but he should make sure that each child understands an equal amount of attention coming from him. After all, it's one thing for a child to feel like he or she is at the bottom of the pecking order; it's another to feel like they don't matter enough for dad to give them any attention at all.

Second, communicate well with your children. This means if you have concerns or complaints about them, express them in an appropriate manner that will not cause them to become defensive.

Third, make sure that you help your children to look forward to spending time with you and their siblings. Many parents find themselves doing things rather than letting the kids help with these chores and projects.

Fourth, spend time helping your children to solve problems on their own. This is not a requirement, but it's how a normal dad would behave. If the dad doesn't help his children solve their problems, they will come up with an excuse to get their parents involved in what is under their own control.

Fifth, if you have time and patience to discipline your children, do so by showing them that you are there for them in times of need. Be sure to be patient when it comes to teaching them new skills or emphasizing different practices; make sure that you work on these things with them as they develop their minds and skills.

Sixth, choose your battles wisely when disciplining your children. While you may always want to teach them the importance of respecting their elders as well as waiting their turn and not interrupting others, it is better to show them these things by taking command over these areas when they arise. The father should focus on important lessons that tend to be more valuable and lasting than small discipline issues.

Seventh, treat your children with love and respect like you would want them to grow up and treat you. This means exhibiting patience in even the toughest situations so that they learn this same trait from you at a young age. If your children feel like they have a good relationship with you, they will model many of your positive traits in order to keep it going in the long-term.

A dad has to be the provider, disciplinarian, nurturer, and teacher. He has to love his family and will always want what's best for them. Fathers are also playmates; they won't give in to a child's every whim, but they will spend hours of fun time with their children just because it can be exhausting at times. And fathers must make sacrifices for their family like managing work life balance, finding time for their marriage and spending time with the kids.

A father is also the disciplinarian and the one responsible for teaching the little ones right from wrong. But in a lot of households, this role is shared with their mothers or wives, and it becomes hard to tell who's really in charge. It's observed that men are more likely to hit children as a result of anger or rash judgment and some are just bad at making disciplinary decisions. This is why some parents come together and make crucial decisions for their children, no matter what side each party is on.

Kids are expected to spend hours with their dads, but they don't see them for as much as mothers in the household. Fathers usually have a 'workaholic' personality and tend to be more focused on their job performances, responsibilities in life, and career growth rather than spending time with their families. This is attributed to their work ethics which puts severe pressure on both parties involved. Fathers get tired of all the demands from work and children, so they decide to distance themselves from family life, not wanting to be burdened by it all.

Media portrayals have contributed a lot towards the way men are seen in society today. Men are commonly portrayed as the breadwinners of the family who are expected to be assertive and authoritative but that's only one side of the story. Fathers are also depicted as either a nurturing partner or an uninvolved figure. If they opt for the latter choice, they're bound to get pushed aside by their own children.

A father is not just defined by his DNA but rather his actions for their family. Children can sense if their parents are genuinely into them or not so they will come to terms with it along the way.

Fatherhood is understood as a social construction of fatherhood. This means that the idea of a father is socially created and socially constructed. There are four factors that affect how fathers are portrayed or imagined in society:

The first factor is association with children. Fathers are frequently portrayed as 'significant others of children'. This means that fathers are often portrayed as an important part of the family and children look up to them. The second factor is their age. Fathers are commonly portrayed as an older figure in a family. Fathers who have children younger than them are rare because they may be perceived as immature or less mature. However, if they have children older than them, then they're likely to be viewed more positively. The third factor is their employment. If mothers stay at home and fathers work outside of the home, then it seems less likely that there will be problems with fatherhood. However, if both parents are working outside of the home, then this could mean that they don't spend as much time with their children.

The fourth factor is family structure. There are two types of families: nuclear families and single-parent families. Nuclear families have a stable family structure and are less likely to experience problems with family issues such as divorce or non-involvement between spouses or parents and children. Single-parent families have an unstable structure and tend to have more difficulties in maintaining traditional male roles because fathers have to fill in a mother's role.

The concept of fatherhood is a social construction. This means that the idea of fatherhood has been created socially. These ideas have changed over time as well as depending on the society one lives in. In American society, fathers are very typical, which can be seen in many sitcoms that focus on American families and family values. However, other societies around the world have different kinds of families and their own ways of perceiving fathers, which can be seen through various films and literature from other countries.

One can also see how the idea of fatherhood has evolved in recent years. In the past, it was important for a father to be the main breadwinner of the family. If his wife had a career, then he had to take care of the home and children. However, recently society has been changing and there have been more stay-at-home dads and more working mothers than ever before.

Fathers are frequently portrayed as the patriarchs of families while mothers are viewed as chaotic and disorganized.

The gender differences in parenting are far-reaching and complex. While there has been a push to make parenting gender neutral, this has not had a major impact on the perceptions of mothers and fathers. Many people still believe there is a mother/father dichotomy that regulates the parenting process. This can be seen through several studies that look at how society views mothers and fathers as well as how their roles were defined in the past.

Chapter 3. Raising a Lively Child or Children

There are a lot of different reasons for parents to worry about the well-being of their children. In fact, many parents say they worry all the time and some say it's difficult to stop worrying. Parents often wonder if they're doing enough for their kids and if they're good enough parents.

No one knows what children are like better than parents do, and chances are you've got some really great ideas about how to raise lively children. If you're a parent who's looking to share your valuable insights with other parents or if you're just interested in tips that might be useful for your own family, then this is for you.

What is a lively child?

"Lively" is a word that describes some characteristics of a child. These are characteristics such as someone being healthy, active and wealthy. Being "lively" describes a person who's bright, energetic and loves life. If you want to teach your kids about great wealth and success, but you don't want them to think they are rich or successful, then tell them instead that they are lively. They will be thankful for the kind words you've geared toward them, and they'll become even more energetic from the praise of being good fun people to know!

Lively children want to interact with adults frequently. They seek opportunities to engage with people who are interesting and stimulating and get bored or unhappy when forced to do something that doesn't interest them. When given tasks that are not interesting, they will often attempt to distract those around them by getting a reaction from them- whether positive or negative- and wishes for adults to play along with the idea that he/she has presented. For example, an 8-year-old boy may suggest to his teacher that they should all go outside and play in the rain. The teacher may be caught off guard but will most likely reject this idea.

Lively children may also be fidgety, spontaneous, confident, assertive and adventurous. Lively people typically have a high amount of curiosity which can often lead them to asking questions that they may not fully appreciate the answer to or are not ready for. They are also highly imaginative and creative.

Lively children can be extremely helpful to their parents and teachers on many occasions. Many parents notice that their child is always bringing home interesting facts from school or doing their own research projects on new topics for schoolwork.

Other benefits and advantages of having an energetic child include:

- Comes home from school grinning from ear to ear and gives his parents a great big hug.
- Has an emotional connection to his parents at a young age, making it easier for the child to learn about and communicate with them.
- Lively children are highly creative, so they tend to come up with new ideas that help them get their feet wet in many situations rather than just one.
- They are also able to maintain a positive attitude towards anything, which is not always practical or realistic, but it attracts attention from other people around them.
- Lively children tend to be very resourceful in almost any situation.

- May have a great potential of being a leader.
- Adventurous, fast paced personality helps them get involved in things that can help them grow socially and emotionally such as acting, music, sports, painting, or any other extracurricular activities.
- Lively children are also likely to reach their academic goals because of their motivation to do well from the beginning.
- Some lively children are also very spiritual and can depend on God more than others.
- Children who are more energetic tend to be healthier throughout their childhood and adulthood because their minds stay fresh all the time.

Now, your goal is to encourage your lively children by giving them gifts and money when you can. If you see them acting crazy or loud, you want to give them a gift or money and tell them they are lively. This will encourage your kids because it shows that they are good fun people to know. By giving money or gifts, this makes your active children feel better about themselves. If they feel worthy of having the things that you're giving them, then this will give more energy for them to continue being good fun people. If you are giving gifts or money as a way to gain energy from your active children, then this might just lead to their being more excited about playing and having fun and from that, they'll become lively!

Almost all of the things that parents do can make their children lively, but there are some things that have the greatest impact on children. If you want to raise a lively child, then you need to start acting like one whenever possible. While raising an energetic child is great for the child, it can be dangerous when it comes to teachers or other people who aren't used to seeing energetic kids. If you want to spread your energy to your children, then try doing activities like exercising or doing any other form of activity that will get you moving. You can also join an exercise group and make friends based on the fact that everyone in the group loves being lively! Make sure you do activities that help your child be a great lively person so he or she will always be active and healthy as well.

If you're wondering why being active is good for your children, then it is because they are closer to being fit. If they are fit, then they will be healthier in the future. Being healthy will prevent them from having health problems later on in life, such as high blood pressure or high cholesterol. If your child is an energetic child who is healthy in the present, then he's more likely to be a healthy adult in the future.

If your children have all of these lively characteristics, then they're sure to be great parents themselves one day. You will be able to teach your children how to raise lively kids and you will also help them stay fit and healthy. To teach them how to also be a good person, you can take them on trips or outings with friends. Even though they may not always want to go out with friends, this will help them learn that it's okay to make friends with new people or old people that they haven't met before. If you do this, then your kids will be more active because they will want to spend time with their friends. When they grow up and have children of their own, these ideas can help them have energetic and healthy kids as well.

If you want to raise a lively child who is active and healthy, then make sure he or she has plenty of sleep. This is important because if the child has a lack of sleep, then he or she will be sluggish and unhealthy the following day. If your child doesn't get enough sleep each night, then tell him that he should go to bed early the next day so he can be lively at school or wherever else he has to attend the next day. If you're worried about your child being energetic at school or wherever else he has to go, then encourage him to play with other kids his age. He'll get plenty of energy if he spends time with other kids and he'll be better able to deal with an active classroom. This can also help your child learn how to deal with stress, which will be a great learning experience for him later on.

If you want to raise well-behaved children who are lively, then tell them that they are good fun people to know. This is the best way for them to know what it feels like to be lively because if they hear this often enough, then they'll start thinking this is who they want to become. If they become lively people, then they will be more energetic and active throughout their lives. It will also help them learn to handle stress better as well because it can show them how to take on new activities and feel comfortable being around other people. If your child isn't a good fun person, then don't worry because you can still raise them to be great kids and that means they'll be a good influence on the world later in life.

Some parents tell their children not to make too much noise when they're at home or other places like school or any other place where there are other people who aren't used to hearing energetic kids. If you want to raise your children to be lively in every place they go, then you can help them out by letting them know that it is okay to make noise. This will also help them learn how to deal with the fact that they are energetic when they are older because this is a time where they have to be at least a little on the quieter side around adults and older people who aren't used to the energy of kids.

If you want your children to be great kids, then make sure they're always active. They should do something each day that helps promote their fitness and health. They should eat healthy foods as well because this will ensure that they'll have a balanced diet and get enough exercise. They should also spend plenty of time with other kids their age as well because this will give them a chance to interact with others and learn how to get along with lots of people. If you want your children to be lively people, then you should try these things yourself and see if they work the way you'd like for them to.

When your children go out in public, then do everything you can to make sure they're on their best behavior. This will help them know that it's okay to behave when they're around other people. They should learn other things as well though because they can't always be good at everything that they do. They should have hobbies that are fun and something that helps them get exercise too. If you want your children to be great kids, then you should make sure they're active and always being on their best behavior when they're out in public.

Make sure your children are energetic by showing them how to be good fun people and letting them know that being lively is important too. This will make sure they know what it's like to be lively and energetic just like you do today. Let them know that it is okay to be so and try to get as much out of their time as you can. This will help your children learn that being energetic helps them have fun and do all of the things they love so much. If you want your children to be lively, then you should take the time to help them learn how to behave like good fun people and let them know that this is an important quality for kids too.

Chapter 4. Reason Why Dads Get Angry with Their Children

Dads are fiercely protective of their children. It's one of the best things about being a dad! But even when you're doing everything you can to make your child happy — which is most of the time — it can be easy for an irrational rage to strike out of nowhere. That's because children grow up and parent themselves. Dads might get angry with their kids because they don't want them to grow up; or they might not have the patience required for a growing, developing human who doesn't want to eat broccoli and just wants candy; or they might be dealing with personal issues like divorce or unemployment.

Many working fathers are a lot like single moms in this regard. They can't turn their heads for a minute to check on the kids, because they're busy working and making money... and if both parents aren't available, kids need two providers for dinner to start cooking even as they keep watch over the food in the microwave.

Not all dads are like this, of course. Some dads are the very best singers and dancers in the "I'm going to teach you how to dance" class. They make fairies out of broccoli, and they undoubtedly love their children more than anything else in the world. But when other dads and moms get annoyed with their kids' behavior, it's because they're used to doing everything for a kid that needs to be done.

When your child is a toddler, he or she does not need you to cook his meals or take him places or help him stay in bed at night. That's why it's hard for some dads to see why kids need their fathers in the first place.

Being a dad doesn't mean that you have to do everything for your kid — although it may seem like it all the time, because your child needs food and shelter and medical care... and if something bad happens to him, you might be his only chance at survival! A lot of dads don't want to think about any of that when they're staring at the TV or trying to focus on work.

But no matter how hard the job of being a dad can be, it's worth it. Not everyone would do it if they had the choice!

If you are a man, then you know how to fix your mistakes. If you have done wrong to someone, then apologize right away. If you have messed up with anyone or anything that has hurt in any way the feelings of another person, then man up and fix your mistakes; try to avoid those mistakes as much as possible in the future.

Spend time with them, play with them, and educate them. Do not let the responsibilities of life get in the way of that time. You have a lifetime to be a father to those children, but you do not need more time than you have. Make the most of your Father's Day!

Do you know the reason why dads are often frustrated with their kids? There is a lot of negative feedback in the family. As parents, they have to show affection and affection to keep children loving them. But there are some children who do not want to receive any attention from their parents, and they will get angry when people try to show them love. The most important thing that you need to remember is that having a relationship with your child is going slow because it can't happen overnight, but once they open up the door for it, it's all about flipping those lights on.

Be patient and understanding with your kids; this will help you both in achieving a better relationship in the long run.

The key takeaway from this should be: "dads get frustrated too. Sometimes they even get angry." This is the most important lesson for kids to learn. Many kids believe that their anger is what drives their dad's anger. And then, of course, as adults, they wonder why things go wrong and blame themselves. I honestly don't think I could have come to terms with my dad's anger earlier without having this point hammered into my head.

Also - a lot of kids say that they are the only child who gets in trouble or yelled at. When I was a kid and started realizing that it wasn't always me (or my fault) I started telling myself "it must be because I'm the only one who will talk back. I must be a bad kid." The first time I heard that I was like "Yes, you are. You are a bad kid" and to hear the logic behind it I thought it was so right! =D

One last piece of advice: as an older sibling, when you become aware of your dad's anger issues, try to help him find ways to solve the problems and learn from his mistakes. That is the best way for all parties to learn and achieve their goals.

I spent a lot of time trying to figure out why my dad yells at me so often. The above mentioned does a nice job of pointing out some causes. And then, when I got angry, it would make him angrier and we'd have this awful cycle. I would explode at him with my anger...and then he would get even more angry and say hurtful things to me.

Which is why I had to step back from him for a while. The only person that could solve this issue was me...and the only way for me to handle it was by getting help from people who knew about these issues. But if you are in a similar situation as I am and want to avoid this cycle here's what you need to remember:

It's not about you.

You can't change how your dad feels...only he can do that. A lot of my anger would come from the fact that my dad was really mad at nothing. And if I responded with anger, it made him even more mad, and he got even angrier. If I just took a second to breathe, think about how stupid yelling is and then talk rationally with my dad about why I did what I did...I could usually get him to calm down. He wasn't being angry because of me...he was just having a bad day/bad week/bad month etc. Regardless of what he thought of me, I was just a tool in his toolbox that he was trying to use to get through whatever issue he was facing. If it wasn't me, it would have been someone else.

I got the idea to calm down from a book called Flow by Csikszentmihalyi. It talked about how when we find the right mindset to deal with something we are not as stressed out if it makes us uncomfortable because we are still in control of our own lives at that point. I was able to only respond with my words during angry outbursts and not react physically. I was able to get through to him far easier when I talked with him in a way that made him calm down. This made both of us happier, which was the goal.

Don't let it get personal.

This is something that I still struggle with sometimes, but it has gotten easier over time because I've realized how much better off my dad and I are when we talk about this stuff. It's easy to get offended by the things we say to one another when we're angry...especially if it seems like they are attacking who you are as a human being. Instead, ask your dad how he is feeling and what is going on in his life. Is he stressed out? Does he have a bad set of circumstances right now? If you can find out why this happens to him and what he is dealing with then you are in a lot better position to be able to help him.

But if no one ever helped him with this stuff, chances are he hasn't learned how to talk about these things in healthy ways yet. Learning how to do so will only take time...but you can buy your dad some time by offering support and resources when you see him struggling. Maybe even let him know you're willing to listen whenever he needs it...without making a big production about it.

Don't drink and yell at your kid.

This might seem over the top because I'm sure there are plenty of loving fathers who have drank a few beers and then gotten their kids riled up...but my dad is one of those guys that will get drunk and then start to feel sorry for himself. And he will use me as a weapon against himself. That's not the only time he does this, but that is one thing I've seen him do. My dad has had depression issues for a long time...and whenever he drinks, those feelings come back to the surface. He has other issues too but this one is the biggest issue when it comes to his relationship with me. I had a very hard time watching my dad struggle with this.

He would yell and scream at things I didn't understand and most of the time he was not being mean about it...just sharing his feelings out loud.

I've tried to learn to react better to these things because I know how much it hurts him...but I don't want to be a bad person. It's difficult for me when my dad yells at me, but I try not to feel guilty because that's what happens whenever he gets drunk and tries to solve problems in an angry way. I remember one night when my dad was drinking really badly...one thing led to another, and it eventually boiled down into an argument involving us two...and I don't blame him for that. I was young and I had a lot of energy, and he was in a really bad mood.

I didn't have the right to yell back at him...or say anything mean to him. Those were his feelings, and it didn't matter how much I knew he was wrong...he had every right to feel that way. The only thing I could do was walk away from the situation because nothing else was going to make dad feel better...not even my anger or my tears.

Don't touch your kid's butt while you hug them goodbye...I'm not kidding. Don't do that. If you do, someday he will find out about it and it will have a lasting impact on your relationship with him, but I'm pretty sure you already know that...

I know this stuff is so corny...but I felt like all of these things needed to be said..by me...to at least one other person out there who wasn't able to adequately express what I was feeling. And if someone can relate to any of this, then I think this is a good place for that person to start their own blog. Maybe they don't want people to read what they have written because of ties to their families or their children...maybe they fear ridicule or being shamed.... but it's all about finding some common ground.

Chapter 5. Dad's Anger Issues Vs. Mom's Anger Issues

Anger management is a critical issue for all parents, but there are differences between how mothers and fathers handle their anger that can have an impact on their kids. Though they may never know exactly where mom or dad's anger issues stem from, children with mothers who have compulsive disorders face an increased risk of developing compulsive habits themselves- while those with dads who struggle with addiction issues are at risk of developing addictive behaviors in imitation.

Mothers who struggle with compulsive issues are often angry and they are even more likely than fathers to use negative reinforcement with their children. "They tend to get physical in discipline. "They're much more likely to be punitive.

Fathers, on the other hand, are less likely to hit than their partners, but they are more likely to criticize their children. "They tend to get emotional in discipline," Weitzman says. "And it's more likely that they'll criticize the child verbally."

Mothers and fathers differ in how they handle stress as well. "Typically, mothers tend to over-compensate with food," Weitzman says. Fathers are less prone to over-eating because their stress tends to be a little lower. But mothers are more prone to overeating because of their anger issues and avoidant behavior in general.

A lot of people would agree that children cause their parents a lot of trouble and stress. One-way parents can deal with this is by channeling their anger into more constructive means. For example, if mom yells at the kids often for breaking things, she could tell them to stop and clean up after themselves or get them a chore chart to break bad behavior up into manageable tasks. Mom is not whipping out the belt or screaming at the kids just because she's angry! She's trying to teach them right from wrong.

This same idea goes even further when you have dad around. Dad will use his anger on things like playing too loud, leaving messes in the house, or sneaking food away from him. However, if he were to use the same methods on yelling at his kids, they would probably perceive it as abuse or a sign of weakness and would not learn anything from the experience. So parents who experience anger issues need to channel these emotions in a productive way to make sure that their children are growing up right.

It is no secret that there can be a stark difference between how a mother and father react to their children when they are frustrated. Dads are often more vocal when angry, while moms tend to be more withdrawn. And just like the different ways mothers and fathers handle their sons and daughters, the differences in how they express anger also varies depending on whether it's directed towards an adult or child.

The way men and women express their anger can also be affected by their upbringing and the way they saw their parents dealing with conflict when they were younger. A man with a father who frequently yelled at others or lost his temper was likely to carry those traits into adulthood. On the other hand, a woman whose mother withdrew from her when she was upset is likely to repeat that behavior with her own children.

Conversely, those children who had a mother and father who were both able to calmly express their anger are more likely to do the same as adults. Being able to identify what was wrong and what needed to be changed without the screaming and shouting can set a child up for life in terms of how they handle their own anger. Those parents who were more withdrawn with their feelings also taught their children that it was okay not to talk about how they were feeling but rather bottle it up inside.

While it may be difficult for men and women to express their anger in the same way, there are strategies that can help them cope with their frustrations so they can continue functioning at a normal level. When a family member is being unreasonable it helps to remain calm and polite but firm. At the same time, it's important for those who are experiencing anger issues to seek out professional help for they may not be able to change everything about themselves through therapy or self-help books without professional guidance.

Anger is a powerful emotion that can be used for good or worse. People who are angry often feel as though they have the right to feel and act in certain ways that would have devastating consequences in certain situations, but they need to understand the detrimental effects of their anger on themselves and other people. I will discuss how mother's anger towards her children differs from one's father's anger towards his children.

It has been said that when a couple divorces parents create two different kinds of relationships with their kids. The parents may treat each child differently based on their gender, personality, age, and how much time they spend with them. Most people who study the impacts of divorce and child support arrangements agree that this is true. Mother's often treat boys more harshly than girls, especially when their daughter's rebel against them, and fathers often treat their sons more harshly than their daughters, especially when they act out.

It has been said that mothers tend to be angry at their sons for being boys and children rather than being little men. This is because parents are often hoping for a different future for these boys- one where they are held up as role models for their brothers and sisters so that they can turn out to be better men than their parents were. Fathers on the other hand are often angry at their daughters for acting out and testing boundaries with them. Although these girls are not intentionally trying to annoy or upset adults, it is very difficult to help a child who acts out in anger with your son- especially when that son is being disrespectful towards you and his mother.

While mothers are often disappointed when these boys grow up and do not become good men, fathers generally experience much more anger from their daughters when they act out rather than being good women. This is because while mothers have been disappointed because of their sons' behavior, fathers have been disappointed because of their daughters' behavior. Fathers experience much more anger than mothers do when their daughters act out because they have been investing much more time and effort in raising them than mothers do. Fathers often expect their daughters to be the same person who behaved well as a child, but unfortunately, they are not. Therefore, fathers are disappointed and angry at them for acting out when they grow up.

In addition to this, fathers spend much more time and effort interacting with their children than mothers do because mothers are often busy working while listening to their children's problems over the phone or computer. Mothers on the other hand spend much less time engaging in this kind of parenting because they prefer not to interact with their children unless something is wrong with them. Doing this creates a huge gap in the child's mind regarding their parental figures and causes them to manipulate their fathers with fear and distance.

Anger issues between parents and their children have been created because of different parenting styles, expectations, and relationships. Fathers expect to be respected by their daughters because of their position as a man, but when they are not, fathers feel as though they have failed in raising them properly because they cannot control them. Mothers expect sons to be good men who will take care of them when they are old and sick. When these boys grow up to be men who are either irresponsible or abusive towards women, mothers feel as though they have failed as parents or that something is wrong with their sons. Both of these parents have different parenting styles, expectations, and relationships with their children. Both of their anger issues with them also affects their relationship with other family members, causing problems in their interpersonal relationships.

For instance, mothers are often angry at their husbands for not doing more to help them out because of the work they do. Fathers are often angry at their wives for not being able to take care of themselves or pay for things like food and rent on time because she spends too much time working on her laptop or phone. These two families use money to control each other and punish one another by withholding money from each other and withholding food from each other when they were not willing to help one another out with finances. When both families use money to control each other, it creates a cycle of anger that is harmful because of what happens when one family member withholds something from the other.

Mothers are often angry at fathers for not taking care of them or being able to do housework properly because he spends too much time working in his garage or backyard. Fathers are often angry at mothers for not taking care of themselves or being able to take care of their children properly because she spends too much time working on her laptop or phone. They use money to punish one another and withhold things from each other that they needed, such as food, rent, and other financial resources. They also use this method of punishment against their children, which causes more problems between the children and their parents because it is used as a method of control. This cycle of anger continues on into the grandchildren's generation as these two families continue to hold onto these unrealistic expectations of each other.

Parents who do not understand how to live with each other will also pass this cycle of anger onto their children because it is easy for them to find comfort in the role they have been given as a child. It is difficult for them to see their parents as real people who have money problems and that choose to use money as a weapon against each other. They may not want their parents to fight each other if they grow up, but they will still see it in their relationship with one another because it is the only way they know how this kind of thing works.

It is important for families to let go of these old patterns of staying together even when they are not happy together. It will be hard for parents to do this because the idea that breaking up or separating from their children will hurt them is very strong within their minds. It is important for children to have a close relationship with both parents, but it is also important for them to be able to see both sides of the family. When parents do not understand how to live with each other, they will use the same techniques that they were abused with as a child and will pass these abusive traits onto their children in order to manipulate them.

Chapter 6. The Ramifications of Dad's Anger

There are a lot of signs that dad is angry, but for the sake of this, we'll focus on the most obvious ones: yelling, slamming doors and/or breaking objects. Without considering the long-term consequences, it's easy to get swept up in someone else's anger and lash out in return. This can be dangerous for kids both emotionally and physically as their frustration levels increase. If you or your children are concerned about your dad's anger — especially with how frighteningly physical, it is — here are some things to keep in mind.

The roots of dad's anger may come from his childhood, perhaps from a bad relationship with an abusive parent. This means the anger is often both physical and verbal. One of the most important things for you to do is to recognize that dad may not be able to control this behavior. If it is due to some form of mental illness, he will need professional help. Sometimes this is due to alcohol or drug use, and it needs to be addressed immediately. As tempting as it may be, please don't try to intervene on your own without any kind of help or guidance. Dad will need professional intervention through counseling and/or medication if he continues with this kind of behavior.

If you're concerned that your dad's anger is compromising your welfare, then you need to talk to him about it. Remember that sometimes we don't know what we're doing until we hear from others. Ask yourself, is this making things worse? By asking for his honest opinion or advice you can be making a positive step toward getting help for your family and yourself. Sometimes a father needs to be the person who steps in and does something different for a while. This doesn't mean he isn't allowed to express his anger further down the line; he just needs to take into account how what he's saying will affect everyone around him -- including his children.

It's important to remember that you must be the mature one in the situation, and that it's not always easy. Try not to get lost in a cycle of anger yourself. Don't let your frustration at him get in your way. Keep talking about how his anger is affecting you, and what you can do together to fix it. It really does take a village sometimes, even when there are just two people living together.

In some households, it seems like no matter how hard dad tries he can't shake his anger problem. It may be time for him to separate from everyone for a while, including his family. This may sound scary, but separation is actually a very positive thing for some families. You can't force someone to do it on his own; give him time to think about his own options and then consider the pros and cons. If he decides he doesn't want to separate, then there are other things you can do.

Don't let anger be the reason your dad walks away from you. This is a common occurrence in families who struggle with anger issues, and it's important that either you or he address it right away. You don't need to solve the problem yourself; your dad needs professional help if this sort of pattern continues. If your father doesn't think he needs help then you need to consider getting it for yourself. This is a difficult situation to be in and it's important that you know that you are not alone.

You don't need an anger problem to suffer from the consequences of anger. You may have seen him lose his job, or your family breaking apart because of his temper. There are many long-term effects of anger on families, so stay alert for signs that it may be bothering him too. The good news is there is a lot you can do about this; here are some steps to take:

If Dad refuses to get help, it's time for the family to step aside. You need to protect your kids from any physical harm they would experience. Make sure he has money and food, but don't let him inside the house for a few days. This will give him time to come up with other solutions. Don't go back until he has had a chance to think about what he's doing and how it affects everyone else around him.

Don't get angry yourself, even if you're feeling nervous or scared; this is his problem, not yours or your siblings'. Just make sure you protect yourself and each other in the meantime and don't allow yourselves to fall into a pattern of anger. If your dad tries to talk to you about it after some time has passed, be honest with him. Be honest with yourself when you're the one feeling frustrated or unhappy. Try to listen to others who have gone through similar situations, because they can help you realize that there is another way.

Talk to your dad directly if you're afraid of him. Stay calm and be firm in your belief that he needs help. You can say something like, "Dad, I know your angry right now but we need to talk about how this affects both of us. I'm worried because this is a problem for the whole family. I wish you'd get some help and then let's talk about it again later."

If someone besides your dad is acting out with anger issues, then talk to them about it by yourself or together. They are not having as direct an impact on you in this situation, but you can still have something to say about it. It's possible they're getting worse, and you've both been trying so hard that neither of you has been seeing how it's affecting your kids or their kids. You can do something about this as a family, but no one should be putting up with aggression or violent behavior within the home.

Did you know that anger is the most common emotion experienced by parents, and there are documented effects of this emotion on their children? This will explain why it's important for fathers to be in control of their anger, how to normalize it, and how they can avoid its negative impacts on their family.

If you are a dad or any other type of parent struggling with anger issues, read on to learn about what may be going wrong—and what can get better!

Anger is the most common emotion experienced by parents. There is no denying that some people find this frustrating due to its negative consequences like failing relationships or misbehavior. But what is the cause of anger? Is it just a personal problem, or can you treat it like any other emotional state and work on changing it? Or is there a biological cause that may be restricting your freedom to choose how you respond to life's difficulties?

Recent studies have discovered that the majority of people feel angry at least some of the time. And, more importantly, many fathers report experiencing anger more often than mothers. Interestingly, this occurs regardless of whether they are married or not. In fact, men without wife's report feeling angry less frequently than men married or single. This is actually quite interesting because a family unit is said to have the largest influence on control of anger. Is anger something that should be controlled by family? Or is it something that affects both parents, regardless of each individual's marital status?

But what happens when a father becomes angry? How does his child react to this emotion? We will explore the effects of such a situation and how they can be addressed, whether at home or in school. Let's begin by looking at why fathers become angry in the first place . . .

The reasons why some people feel angry are varied. The causes of anger are most often the result of poor relationships with family and friends, past negative experiences, or a predisposition to respond to certain situations in a particular way. So, while anger is a normal emotion that many people experience from time to time, the situations that trigger it are not. Additionally, our brain's control of behavior is guided by learned habits. And the way our brain responds to stimuli can be changed over time by new experiences.

In fact, many people discover a biological link between anger and serotonin levels in the brain. Serotonin is said to be a "feel-good hormone." It works in the brain's frontal lobe by regulating your moods, sleep patterns, appetite, and pain sensitivity, just to name a few things. It also plays a significant role in controlling your behavior and responses to certain situations and stimuli. So if serotonin levels are low or absent, anger can result as well as other problems such as anxiety disorders or depression symptoms.

Anger has both positive and negative impacts on personal development. So, is it always bad?

It's true that anger can be a problem when it becomes destructive, especially in the case of physical violence. But this does not mean that anger is always bad. In fact, anger can have a positive effect at times. For example, anger might be helpful in situations where someone has to stand up for their rights or where we feel morally frustrated and need to defend our opinions and beliefs. This type of behavior can motivate us to act responsibly and improve our relationships with others in society. It also motivates us to "fight" against unjust laws or unfair practices.

Additionally, anger might alert you to a certain situation or problem you need to fix. For example, if you are angry that your child is not doing their homework, perhaps there is something else going on that requires your attention. Or if you're angry at your spouse for being lazy around the house, it may be because they aren't doing what they are supposed to do. In both cases, there are issues that require immediate attention and solutions before it becomes a bigger problem.

How can dads control anger?

Still, there are also many ways to control anger in the long-term involving positive behaviors and changes in attitude and belief system. If you are a father who finds himself feeling angry more often than he or others would like, here are some tips for controlling your anger in the right way.

Say what you mean and mean what you say. First, decide if what you're saying is really true or if it's just another way to express anger. If it's the former, then think before you speak. And always choose your words wisely because they have the power to offend someone else or damage a relationship. In fact, the strongest relationships are made by couples who take time to express themselves openly and honestly with each other.

There's that good advice again! Do some stretching before going to bed if time allows (and in between classes if you're on a tight schedule) ... It will help you wind down and relax while also helping you relieve any muscle tension that may have built up during the day. It's like a warm hug from your bed!

Chapter 7. How Dads Cope Up With Anger Towards their Children

Parenting is a full-time job, and that's without the necessity of being an attentive person. Being a dad, in particular, comes with its own set of special challenges.

There are many ways for fathers to cope with anger they may feel towards their children. Sometimes anger comes with outbursts, while others may be accompanied by other feelings. These include blaming themselves and trivializing their children's faults. There are also those who resort to abusive treatment, which is not something a dad should ever go down too.

Although dads can come up with many approaches for dealing with the most difficult moments in parenting, there are others that work well.

Blaming oneself is something that many fathers do. This is especially during the first few months of their kids' lives, especially those who are new to parenting. With this approach, there are so many emotions to deal with, and these include anger mixed with guilt.

Some parents also tend to trivialize their children's faults because of which anger towards them comes, but this is a wrong approach to be taken by dads. This brings out the wrong interpretation of what they've actually done, making them feel that they're not really capable as parents.

A third approach dads take involves using abusive treatment towards their children. Although this can be done intentionally on a hostile basis, it can also happen accidentally.

The most effective approach for dealing with anger is to understand why it exists. Each of these approaches mentioned above are common, and they work for some dads who are experiencing a difficult time. It's just that understanding each of these approaches can help bring about an appropriate reaction towards them, instead of doing the wrong way. By doing this, the role of being a dad will be easier to manage.

For those who need further assistance on parenting, there are people who can provide quality advice and support for them. This is also possible through online platforms where helpful material related to parenting is made available for everyone's needs and concerns in mind.

Sometimes parents just can't control their anger towards their children. But the question is, how do they cope up with it? That was the question I asked myself when I found out that my wife and one of our kids were going to experience some pretty tough times. I knew there was no way on earth I could keep my feelings in check, so to help her out and ease our son's mind, we had to find a way to reach him—before he did something regrettable.

There are many ways you can find relief from an existential problem like this: meditation, exercise, talking with friends or loved ones, diet changes—the list goes on and on.

Where anger starts, anxiety always follows. And when you get familiar with this cycle, like most people who suffer from anxiety, you make the mistake of assuming that if you're not anxious all the time then you don't have any reason to feel anything at all. In other words, there's nothing wrong with me; it must be something else in my life that makes me feel bad.

These thoughts are natural enough, and it's in a person's best interest not to gratify the anxiety that provokes negative thoughts, but when you feel chronically anxious about something and won't let go of it, you're not doing yourself any favors.

In a world where fathers are taught to be tough and unemotional, coping with anger towards their children is not always an easy feat. Learn how you can cope up with these pent-up frustrations, as well as what the benefits of such an ability can result in.

Have you ever felt like there's no way out of your past mistakes? You're stuck in a never-ending spiral that only leaves you feeling more resentful towards your child? Fear not, because this is going to explain how to get over these feelings and still be the happiest father on earth.

However, let me first start by explaining what it means to be an empathetic father and why it is so important. Empathy is what makes us human beings. It's the natural ability to put ourselves in someone else's shoes and try to understand their feelings and perspectives. It helps us trust one another and make more personal connections. I believe that empathy plays such a big role in parenting because it allows you to love your child with all your heart, even when you are having the most difficult of times communicating with them.

According to experts, empathy is developed through three main factors: genetics, parenting style and the environment in which the child grows up in. I'm sure you already know how difficult parenting can be, but there are factors out of our control that also influence our ability to connect with our children. These include the mental health issues and behavioral disorders that we may have developed before we were even born.

Though empathy is something that is very much out of our control, feeling anger towards our children is a completely different matter. Anger is the opposite of empathy because it makes us react rashly without even considering what the other person feels about it. In a way, anger can be a form of defense mechanism- we feel angry because we think that it will keep us from feeling hurt or sad. However, it can also mean that we are trying to mask our own insecurities and feelings of being inferior to others.

To put things more simply, anger is reactive emotion and empathy is proactive one. Anger is like an automatic reflex reaction, while empathy involves pausing for a moment and putting yourself in someone else's shoes.

Anger has different causes, including genetics (as with any other negative emotions) as well as life experiences. We tend to incorporate our parents' behaviors into our lives eventually because we don't have any other mentors at such a young age. In the same vein, we may also get frustrated with our child because they are being lazy or stubborn (which are results of a lack of patience), but there is a way to react to this without losing control.

Most empathetic fathers know that anger means fighting against your own feelings. It is an emotion that allows us to attack our children in ways that aren't truly justified by what has happened. We might even lash out in ways that we wouldn't normally do to something else, like punching the wall or slamming doors in order to "get it out". However, you can learn how it feels for your child to feel angry and how you can express your frustrations towards them differently so that it will be more effective.

In order to do so, you need to approach your child with empathy and not anger. You need to put yourself into their shoes and ask questions about the problem- what are they feeling? What would make them feel better? What do they think about the situation? By not reacting to your child's anger by saying something really hurtful or by hitting them, you open a real dialogue that will be key in helping you move past this point.

But what if your child doesn't want to talk it out with you? This is absolutely fine, because sometimes children just need time alone in order to reflect on their actions and feelings. This is really important because, in order to get over the problem, they need to come to terms with what they have done wrong in the first place.

I understand that it is very easy to feel angry towards our children when they act out and do things that we don't like, especially if it means putting their own safety at risk. Of course, all children have their own flaws and there are no perfect kids out there (not even yours), but you need to remind yourself that you're not going to be around forever, and this stage of parenting will eventually be over. This means that you won't always have the right or responsibility of shaming and punishing your child for their wrongdoings. Just remember that every child has their own learning curve, and you shouldn't let your own frustration with them get to you.

So, what do we do in order to get over our anger towards our children? This is a very difficult question to answer, especially when your child has just disappointed you so much. However, the first step towards doing this is realizing that they are never going to be perfect. We need to become parents that recognize the good in our child and not always the bad and use it as an excuse for being angry all the time.

A lot of things in parenting just have to be learned through experience- it takes time before we can begin seeing true results from our efforts at nurturing children emotionally as well as physically. This means that you have to be patient with yourself and continue doing what you're already doing.

Raising kids isn't something that can be learned in a week or even in a few days. It's something that is going to take a lifetime, and it's very important to remember this because otherwise, your children can grow up into adults who don't respect you at all.

Although Dads might be able to avoid the anger, many of them feel unable to keep their frustration in check. Studies show that boys tend to become more aggressive as they mature and learn how to cope with their emotions, especially if they come across tough rules or strong criticism from their parents

It can be difficult for a father with a restless, demanding child and he becomes frustrated when the child is not following his instructions or trying his best. Many psychologists state that fathers are even more prone to yelling at children because it is simply what men do. The phrase 'he doesn't listen' can trigger this impulse. However, it is essential that the father learns how to contain his anger and use it constructively.

'How To Deal with The Anger Caused By Your Children'

As already mentioned before, there are many ways to avoid the anger and frustration caused by your children. If you have the ability to see the things from your child's perspective, then you will understand why some of them behave so stubbornly. If parents feel frustrated when their children are not listening, then they should use this feeling to understand and communicate with their kids in a better way. At times, parents may feel like yelling at their child, but they should calm down first and try to talk calmly. If there is no other option but to yell, then it would be better if they do it in private.

Despite all of the advantages mentioned above, it is still important to make sure that the child learns how to deal with their anger. This will help them grow up in a healthy way and have a good relationship with their parents. It is also important that they are able to understand why their parent was angry with them, what should they do instead and use this knowledge to improve in the future.

Chapter 8. Controlling Dad's Angry Outbursts

There are many ways to deal with anger. The first step is to admit that anger can occur. Next, confront your feelings and admit that you're angry and work on understanding why this feeling of anger is important for you. This is just the start of the process, and these steps will help you understand how Anger works in your life so that you feel less out of control and more explanatory about how it impacts your life.

All too often we end up feeling as though our emotions are completely out of our control which leads to an increase in frustration because we can't predict when this emotion will happen next, what triggers it or how long it may last for. This will help to explain how anger works in your life and how to cope with these feelings.

The next step is to find a way of dealing with the anger and minimizing the feelings of frustration that accompany this emotion. Given the abuse we experience on a daily basis it's hardly surprising that we might feel angry quickly, but what happens when we're left feeling frustrated or downright annoyed? This is where it's important to differentiate between anger and frustration. It's important to remember that when you feel angry you can control it and you're not going crazy or psychotic, however when you feel frustrated you cannot control your emotions and they can happen 'out of nowhere'.

When it comes to parenting, dads are expected to be strong and in control. It's a tall order, but being a dad is hard work. And when tensions run high or if they feel like they are constantly being underappreciated, fathers might feel as though they have no control of their anger.

That's why we put together on how dads can manage their anger - whether it be with their kids or when he feels like he is unfairly judged by his spouse.

Often when parents are in conflict, they respond by withdrawing into the children, or lashing out at their spouse or partner violently, and losing all sense of dignity and respect. This is particularly true of fathers who in a heated moment can either be overly harsh or emotional, or who might even lash out physically.

It's not uncommon for fathers to lose their temper, both at home and at work, and as a result become more aggressive and edgy. But fathers also have a higher tendency than mothers for aggression and should take extra steps to manage their anger before it gets the best of them.

If you are prone to anger, there are some effective techniques that you can use to keep yourself in check when your emotions get the better of you.

It's important to understand that anger is both natural and normal; most people experience it occasionally. It's when the anger becomes out of control that it's a problem.

Plenty of men suffer from severe anger issues because they don't take any steps to deal with their anger. They either suppress their feelings of anger, which can lead to anxiety and depression, or they act on their impulses in violent ways, or both.

If you have a problem with losing your temper, you need to take action to change things right away. Take this opportunity to learn how you can temper your exacting nature so that you don't get into trouble with yourself and others around you.

The most important thing to remember is that it's perfectly natural to not always be in control of your feelings. You may experience anger or frustration. It's how you deal with those feelings that is important.

1) Don't get angry. When someone makes you angry, don't respond with anger in kind - just try to keep calm as best as possible. Just tell yourself in your mind that it's okay to feel and act angry, but recognize that if you respond in anger, things are going to get a lot worse.

2) Think before you speak. When you are angry try not to say things that you'll regret later. Typically, people who lose their temper say very hurtful things because they can't think straight when they're angry. So just take a moment before you speak and ask yourself if what you're about to say is worth saying. You might even consider keeping a diary about things that you said when you lost your temper. Then, after you've had time to think over your actions, you can use what you wrote as a reminder of how not to act.

3) Take deep breaths and count to ten. It can be very upsetting when someone starts to argue with you, especially if it's the same thing over and over again. So just take a few calming breaths before you respond. This will give you the opportunity to control yourself instead of being controlled by your feelings.

4) Focus on how you're feeling. When you are feeling angry, you might not be thinking too clearly. Take some time to calm yourself and focus on your anger by using the "5 S's:

S - Stop - No one can reason with someone who's angry and treating them like they're crazy. Trying to talk to such a person will just make things worse because they aren't in a rational state of mind. So just stop them from saying anything that will aggravate you further. Don't react with anger, don't yell, and don't call names - just wait until they cool off enough to hear what you have to say calmly.

S - Stand up - Anger flares when you are sitting down, because it seems as if you're a cornered victim. Standing up will show the other person that you are not afraid and will give them a chance to calm down too.

S - Smile - If you've been frowning at the world around you, it might be a good idea to smile. Smiling will help you see things from a different perspective and calm yourself down.

5) **Write it down.** When you feel that your anger is gaining control over your actions, write the problem in a diary or journal so that you can't say anything you'll regret later without facing what you have said immediately. You may not think you have a problem, but once you are forced to confront your actions on paper, you may be surprised at the emotional roller coaster ride your words will put others through.

6) **Set up a distraction.** If you find yourself about to lose your temper, try whistling or cleaning something in order to delay reacting until later. Distractions are better than giving in to anger because they give you time to cool down and realize that your anger is way out of proportion. You can always go back later and address the issue with a cooler head (and far fewer expletives).

7) Don't react while angry. Anger often leads people to make impulsive statements or actions that they will regret later. So, if you find yourself about to say something inappropriate while angry, try to wait until you have calmed down before making your remark.

8) Get some perspective. If you find yourself losing your temper regularly, remember that the other person has no way of knowing how much it upsets you or the repercussions it could have for him/her. Chances are he/she doesn't have a clue what is really bothering you and so is probably genuinely upset by your actions. There's no need to sulk or lash out at the person because they don't know. Giving them a break may help get things back on track and prevent anger from getting out of hand with potential ruinous consequences later on.

9) Be patient. Hopefully, your partner has been working hard on trying to change their behavior and/or their thinking. You may have to be patient and give them time to get the hang of it. The first step may take awhile but each subsequent step should be easier. Don't expect immediate results and don't pressure them into doing things sooner than they are ready or able. It's important that they try to do things correctly without worrying about how long it takes them. Some people figure this out for themselves, others need a little prodding.

10) Never lose your temper with children. Even if they did something wrong, never allow yourself to lose control of your anger at a child. Children usually don't even know they are doing anything wrong and will likely turn out just fine in life. The wise man once said, "Children are our future."

11) Avoid conversations that might lead to arguments or violence. These include topics such as politics or religion. Arguing about a disagreement may make things worse than you think it will. Do not argue with your spouse over the phone or on the Internet; this sort of communication is a good way to spark an argument and get you angry instead of them.

No pressure - just read the first few sections and see if anything clicks. If not, skip ahead to the end of this where we'll talk about how you can get more support for controlling your anger.

How do I know if I'm having an angry outburst?

-Excessive yelling, yelling in frustration while doing mundane tasks, angry outbursts in the car or at the grocery store, yelling when walking or shaking hands, or more subtle signs like an angry tone of voice during conversation.

-Your attitude changes from friendly to angry quickly and without warning. You never are a happy person but for some reason you seem to switch to this "off" person that only gets mad. It's not a pleasant thought but it's true. This is why your teen may be struggling so much with acting out, being defiant, and killing animals - you are not teaching them that they should be nice to others and not get into fights.

-With this in mind, let's talk about what you can do to control your angry outbursts.

Here are some of the negative side effects of anger:

-It causes stress and will shorten your life by 4 years

-An angry person is more likely to suffer from heart attacks and strokes.

The last thing you want to be doing when you are having an angry outburst is stressing out your body. This will lead to heart problems and life shortening. When you are experiencing this anger issue, see where you can start by not yelling or being rude with other people, especially if they are smaller than you or younger than you. Talk calmly instead of yelling and being disrespectful.

What are you doing that is making you feel so angry? Try to find creative ways to cope with your stress instead of yelling at people. This can include exercising, reading a book about the benefits of meditation, watching a movie that makes you laugh, etc. Get creative if you do not know what else to do!

It is more than OK to have a bad day here and there. Everyone does - it's part of being human. However, being violently angry all the time will not allow for any progress in your personal life or with helping out your children. Take steps to control your anger now.

Chapter 9. Guide to Anger Management Regimen

The choice to discipline your children is not one you should take lightly. However, if you feel that your anger is controlling you and impacting negatively on the parent-child relationship, it may be time for anger management. You can take charge of your situation and lead a happier life with some simple techniques.

If you find yourself feeling angry or irritable on a regular basis, it might be time to take a look at your anger management regimen. In order to prevent anger and other related negative emotions from overtaking what should be a happy life, it is best to have an outlet for those feelings. This will give you some great tips on how to develop an effective anger management regime!

How do you form a Regimen?

First off, you need to have some sort of general idea of how you want your regimen to work. In most cases, this will be based around a time schedule. Particular times throughout the day or week will be set aside for specific types of activities that will help you release the negative emotions associated with anger. In order to make it all fit into your schedule, you will need to have a sense of how much time each activity should take.

Here are some helpful tips to start an anger management regiment:

-Find a designated place to chill out when you're angry – like a bedroom, bathroom or outdoor shed – before dealing with kids when they have done something wrong. This helps in two ways: it prevents the negative effects of rage from spreading around your household and allows you to focus on correcting the problem before continuing on with work or play without distractions.

-Do not hesitate to set clear guidelines and consequences for children. Never start off by saying something like, "I'm really angry with you." Start off calmly, giving your child a clear explanation of what is expected and how the situation can be avoided in the future.

-Know when to say when! If you are constantly expressing your anger at the kids, it may be time to chill out and consider other ways of reaching a resolution or teaching the kids proper behavior. If you find that there is no end in sight to your anger, seek professional help.

-You may want to enlist the help of a mental health professional or counselor. This person will help you work through any psychological issues that are causing your anger. An anger management session with a therapist will allow you to express your emotions in a safe environment and will fill you with peace of mind knowing that you are not mad at the 'cure.'

-Acknowledge and accept that others may also have strong feelings about things in your life. Pay attention to those signs of frustration and dish out some tough love when necessary. One thing parent should never do is try to sweep things under the rug and pretend that nothing is wrong. This will only hurt your relationship with the child.

-You should never be angry at a child for expressing their anger and frustration. If they can't handle the situation on their own, you are not helping them out by becoming their disciplinarian. Instead, some good advice may be needed - maybe a new rule about going to bed or having to clean up after themselves.

-If you find that your anger is getting out of hand - like punching holes in the wall or biting furniture - enlist the help of your partner or spouse if you can; tell them about your anger. Being angry with someone like your child is not something that should be hidden - say something!

-Never let anger drive you. You may lose sight of your emotions and act without thought, or you could end up hurting the child in some way, making them angry at you. This is a very serious thing to do - one that could lead to a lot of problems later on in life.

-Do not yell at other people for anger management issues - it's just going to make things worse! If you don't want to deal with them, get a babysitter or engage in another activity. Wait until things calm down before trying to talk to someone who may need a friendly word.

-Be careful with using the term "hate." If you find yourself calling your child names, asking how you can hate them, or making any other comments that hint at this emotion, it may be time to reconsider your behavior.

-If you have been drinking alcohol or engaging in any substance abuse, stay away from kids for a while. You need to deal with this issue first before making your children face the consequences of your bad decisions. People indulge in these behaviors for different reasons - like depression or frustration with life – so try to address these issues by getting help and not by lashing out at someone else.

-Meditations can serve many purposes in helping you deal with your negative feelings about anger. One important purpose is to give yourself a calming environment in which to relax and enjoy yourself while also getting rid of some negative energy from your body. While there are many different types of meditation, one of the most popular is transcendental meditation.

This can be especially helpful for people with anger management issues, especially if they have difficulty dealing with the negative emotions associated with angry behavior.

In order to make meditation a part of your rage management regime, you should first find out how long it takes for you to relax when meditating. If it takes only a short period of time, then there is no problem in incorporating other activities into your rage management regimen. However, if it takes a long time, you might have to make room for it in your schedule.

-Exercise is another helpful avenue for releasing anger and other negative emotions. Studies have shown that exercising regularly can help lessen feelings of anger and irritability. This makes exercise an ideal activity to include in your rage management regimen. You should select a type of exercise that you enjoy doing, because this will help you stick with it. If you don't like the activity, you will probably not do it as often as is needed for optimal results.

-A great tool for managing your anger is journaling. Even if you do not have any specific problems at the moment, there are always general feelings of negativity that we experience from time to time. Journaling is an excellent way of voicing those emotions and getting them out of your system. It also helps pinpoint those times when your anger has gotten out of hand, so that you can make adjustments to better deal with it in the future.

-Writing letters can be another effective method of dealing with negative emotions associated with anger and rage. You might find the experience of writing letters a more cathartic than journaling. Whatever method you choose, make sure that you do your writing during scheduled times in order to adhere to your schedule.

-Meditation can also be incorporated into your meditation schedule time. You might try meditating first thing in the morning, or even before bed at night. As mentioned above, this is an excellent tool for helping you relax and get rid of some of the negative energy that builds up while dealing with everyday life.

It is best to have some knowledge about what activities are most helpful to you for venting anger and other negative emotions. Doing so will help you choose appropriate activities to fit them into your schedule as well!

Which Activities Are the Best for Anger Management?

There are many activities that you can use while venting personal anger. Following is a list of possibilities that should help give you an idea of which ones should be included in your regimen:

As you can see, there are many different ways to release anger and other negative emotions. With proper practice, all of these options can become second nature and completely replace the need for more destructive methods in dealing with negative emotions. In fact, you will probably find that these activities can actually help you to better deal with your negative emotions!

If you are facing issues with your anger management and you feel like it is affecting yourself and your family, be sure to seek help. There are many other types of counseling that can help manage your emotions and deal with the underlying issues.

Although anger can be a healthy response to protect oneself when threatened, it is important to control this powerful emotion and take actions that counteract negative thoughts with positive ones. A good anger management regimen includes identifying triggers of your anger and taking steps to avoid them, such as avoiding confrontations or asking others for advice before acting.

It is important to have an Anger Management Regimen in order to help you understand your emotions better and make positive changes in your life. This is important because many people have an assumption that since the body releases endorphins after experiencing an intense feeling it is impossible not feel happy all of the time. This assumption is false because it only makes the individual feel like they are not capable of controlling their emotions.

Conclusion

As we all know, the world has been trapped in a never-ending downward spiral of escalating anger and intolerance, with many people opting out of society. However, it's not just others that should be scared about the potential ramifications of perpetual rage - it's our daddies!

Nowadays, anger management for dads is becoming increasingly necessary to maintain healthy relationships with children and family members alike. This provides tips on how to avoid these toxic emotions while maintaining your cool; learning new and healthy ways to express yourself; recognizing what triggers you; exploring the role that fatherhood can play in your life ; and even having some fun along the way! Consider this essential knowledge for keeping everyone safe.

It may seem difficult to believe that we, as modern men, act out of anger in the first place. While we may not realize this at first, our fathers are more likely to take it out on us than anyone else in the family. As a result, daddies can develop a somewhat jaded view of what society deems acceptable for a dad. This is not the best way to build trust and respect between you and your children - making us less likely to play nice with them (or anyone else) in the first place.

When you have trouble expressing yourself or are prone towards anger at any given time, practicing these tips on anger management for dads will greatly benefit you. It may seem difficult at first, but with practice, you will see big improvements in your relationships with those you love.

The key to managing anger and anxiety is to identify the source of the negative feelings before they get out of hand.

The first, and arguably most important step to managing anger, is learning what makes you angry. Anger management for dads means understanding which situations are likely to make you mad, as well as which personal characteristics are more likely to bring about your rage. It's also important to understand that no one is perfect in their anger management abilities – everyone has bad days where it seems like they can't do anything right or stop the ticker tape of self-criticism from sounding in their head.

Understanding which factors make you angry will help you develop strategies for coping with these feelings. Relaxation techniques are often effective ways of calming pent-up anger and releasing negativity through deep breathing exercises or meditation techniques.

It's important to create a plan for managing anger that you really believe in because one of the most common mistakes made by those who feel angry is believing that they can just "walk away" from the situation they are angry at. The truth is, anger management for dads is much more than just walking away. If you really want to get rid of anger, it's best to man up and do something about it – a simple letter expressing your feelings might be enough to calm some folks down.

One other thing I'd like to mention is that although writing down how you feel can help calm your emotions, this isn't going to do anything about the underlying problem causing you anger in the first place. For example, if you're more likely to be angry during a long car ride in the winter, the ticketed may want to do something about that situation. After all, anger management for dads is as much about understanding which situations are likely to cause you anger as it is about being proactive about preventing them.

What to do: Man Up – The first step in managing anger is realizing that it's happening at all. Acknowledge your feelings and then take action to control or change whatever caused you angst in the first place.

"Understanding which factors make you angry will help you develop strategies for coping with these feelings." This is a key step in the transformation from an angry, abusive man to a loving and emotionally strong father. While I don't have any problem understanding why I'm angry, one of my biggest challenges is overcoming my instinctive reactions to overwhelming situations.

"Relaxation techniques are often effective ways of calming pent-up anger and releasing negativity through deep breathing exercises or meditation techniques." I'm lucky to know that I can take a deep breath and calm myself down whenever I need to, but it takes tremendous focus to do so. For most men, the pressure of being a father is like a boiling cauldron – because they're under such tremendous stress, they can't even think straight.

It can take some effort to learn how to control your emotions. I've experienced an extreme reaction in the past when my wife told me that she was pregnant – that reaction is what caused me to train for and run the NYC Marathon. It can also take some effort to learn certain coping mechanisms that don't involve screaming or hurting people.

What NOT to do: Don't hit someone when you're angry – "I'm sorry… I'm just really stressed out."

Don't say you're sorry and then keep doing something wrong. It's simply not enough.

Avoid Re-victimizing Yourself– "I just can't understand why she didn't tell me this before, why she waited so long, etc…" Even though my wife is the one who did the infidelity and the lying in the beginning, I lost all respect for her after she told me about it by saying things like this. I want to be there for my wife, and I want her to feel secure that I'm not going to leave her. We didn't talk for months after the baby was born because she was so mad at me, and I felt like it wouldn't help anything if we talked.

What you NEED to do instead: Sit down and figure out a solution that both of you can agree on. Good communication is a huge key in dealing with anger.

All of us go through periods where we lose our temper with our children, spouses, friends, or anyone else. In specific situations, it's important to learn how to manage anger in ways that don't endanger you or anyone else – for example, if you feel like you're going to lose it on the road, pull off and try taking a few deep breaths before doing anything rash.

"Research has shown that men are significantly more likely to act out in anger than women."

An interesting thing about anger management for dads is that it can be difficult for a man to figure out most of these techniques on his own. In fact, research has shown that men are significantly more likely to act out in anger than women. For this reason, some experts recommend finding a support group for help with coping with intense emotions.

"Social support is a key component in healthy coping strategies."

Another thing I've noticed is that the only way I can keep my anger in check is by opening up to others about the difficulties I'm having. That's why it's so important for dads to find at least one or two people that they can trust with their problems and talk things over with on a regular basis.

What NOT to do: Don't stew inside – even if you're angry at yourself, don't keep your distance from the rest of the family.

Don't hold back your emotions – don't bottled up your feelings and then let them out later on. The longer you wait to deal with your problems, the harder it can be for them to go away.

Avoid feeling guilty – "At least I'm not doing this to my kids." Guilt gets us into trouble in many different ways. One of the biggest strategies for coping with anger is knowing how to identify and avoid being victimized by guilt.

What you NEED to do instead: Re-engage with the rest of your family. Try to see how you can help them and be there for them. Don't let guilt cause a wedge between you and your partner or kids, because ultimately it will cause more harm than good for everyone in your life.

Ask yourself these three questions when you're tempted to act out in anger…Who will I feel guilty about hurting? Am I more important than my family? Or, am I more important than myself?"

"Accept that our anger is part of who we are, at least as long as we're alive. Anger is a universal, normal, and natural emotion."

In conclusion, anger management is a valuable asset for any father. It can be beneficial to their relationships and mental and physical health as well as simplify the parenting process. In addition, anger management can allow for better empathy and potentially reduce aggressive behavior in children.

www.ingramcontent.com/pod-product-compliance
Lightning Source LLC
Chambersburg PA
CBHW070642120526
44590CB00013BA/828